PRAISE FOR UNHOMEWORK

This book offers an inspiring alternative to the setting of homework for homework's sake. Mark shows us how to turn the sometimes dubious exercise of ritual homework-setting into a genuinely useful and positive experience. He demonstrates how homework can play a significant role in pupil progress, so that it is no longer seen as a bolt-on activity by learners or their teachers.

Written in a lively and accessible way, Mark's theory of Unhomework makes differentiating for every learner both simple and tactful. His innovative approach is sensitive to all three faces of the homework experience – learner, teacher and parent.

Isabella Wallace, education consultant, author and presenter, founder and managing trustee of Reach Out 2 Schools

---

Unhomework furnishes a philosophy for all primary and secondary teachers with a reliable array of homework tactics, resilience and thought. This book re-kindles the value of home-learning and fosters the process from a creative-curricular experience. This completes the perfect homework utopia. Using project-based learning, Creasy shuns the traditional homework-setting and chasing methods and shares his epiphany millisecond (which you may also have experienced) that transformed his thinking about homework altogether! *Unhomework* promotes inspiring, well-thought-out and differentiated homework that has stirred my own practice. This will add value for all individual teachers and students alike in any school and, in reading this book, you will secure a classroom experience that lowers teacher-workload, yet heightens student grit and independence.

Creasy showcases 'enquiry within a context'; learning beyond the classroom and equipping students to think, in order to take responsibility for themselves to increase rewards both emotionally and intellectually. He quite rightly berates the worksheet and advocates self-selecting timeframes and missions. *Unhomework*, full of intrinsic values to shift school policy, has thoughtful analogies: 'When I do good, I feel good. When I do bad, I feel bad!' In a nutshell, *Unhomework* is the passport to 'free children from the straightjacket of standardised homework'. I cannot wait to get back into the classroom to mutate my plans from homework to Unhomework. A brilliant read that I want to devour all over again!

Ross Morrison McGill, teacher and author of *100 Ideas: Outstanding Lessons*

I was hooked from the off, as the book was inspired by a child's comments, not dreamt up due to government reform or an Ofsted checklist – although I am sure it would satisfy both. Mark draws on many sources, from Pablo Picasso to Vicky Pollard, yet it is children who have clearly been his defining teachers and inspiration throughout.

I continued with a wry smile as another savvy pupil exposed the flaws in setting traditional homework, only completing it when he thought it was for his benefit not the teacher's – 'Sneaky!' Like any good educational book, this held up a mirror to my own practice and made me question whether I was merely obeying the homework policy, checking that task off and moving on the learning, without allocating quality time for children to reflect. Am I allowing opportunities for them to develop and show off their strengths as they complete homework, or just confirming what I already know?

Mark continually reinforces the need for consistency and trust in the children, with his philosophy of the 5Rs at the heart. The students can then take responsibility for their own learning with the teacher as the trusted 'guide at the side'; 'unGoogleable' tasks are set but the teacher is there to support children as they wrestle with their own insecurities or fear of failure.

I loved reading the personal and shared successes through scripted anecdotes, particularly where children had surprised themselves, their teachers and/or their parents. Also, the wonderfully moving tales of pupils empowering each other through praise and constructive criticism, modelled by their 'guide at the side': children hailing their peers as the motivation to challenge themselves further, 'I didn't know what I could do until I saw others doing it – they inspired me.' It is child-led learning at its most powerful, as they set the timeframe and success criteria, which they can then use to assess against. And it will be completed because they want to – they understand the responsibility that this freedom brings.

Now is the perfect time to reflect on your own practice as educational policy puts homework back into the hands of head teachers. Unhomework is purposeful and stimulating, a chance for children to develop their learning skills whilst exploring the new knowledge-heavy curriculum: this is truly a platform for children to prepare socially and emotionally for the unknown challenges of the twenty-first century.

Unhomework addresses how to involve everyone – I will be sending out Mark's list of how parents can help develop their child's learning skills at home and adding my own. There are even examples and resources to help practitioners, from NQTs to head teachers, get started. Again I was moved at how the children had inspired colleagues and convinced parents, as a unit, using the 5Rs; a personal reminder to share my own and my class's successes, not by preaching but ensuring I don't become an 'educational Gollum'.

Ruth Saxton, primary teacher, AST in creativity and chair of the National Association for the Teaching of Drama

---

Avoiding stagnation at all costs, and maintaining an enviable passion for children and the learning process, Mark Creasy is a teacher who thinks outside the box, outside the classroom and outside the norm. He transcends the perimeters of the classroom walls and takes his students with him! Fanatical about teaching and learning, he endeavours to make learning exciting, meaningful and memorable for the students. He seeks strategies that give his students opportunities to investigate real-world knowledge, taking learning to the next action-packed level. Think maverick innovation, the unexpected, movement-oriented and a little bit crazy ... then you'll be on the right track.

Both as a teacher and a parent in daily contact with adolescents, I believe the ability of young people to engage in rigorous analytical thinking, creativity and problem-solving has been eroded. It would seem to me that Mark's *Unhomework* addresses all of these skills. *Unhomework* stresses that the role of a teacher is crucial in not only guiding young learners in their search for information, but also in providing the tools to evaluate the usefulness and veracity of that information and to formulate their own thoughts and arguments on the basis of it. At a time when a curriculum and exam-driven education system straitjackets even the most dynamic teacher, so that schemes of work and lessons often become stifling and not stimulating, *Unhomework* inspires the practitioner not only to facilitate thinking skills and PLTS but also to build in opportunities for young learners to become creative, critical thinkers: room to make lots of mistakes, to build resilience and to know *how* to learn anything they choose to. *Unhomework* emphasises the need to give all young people a huge 'toolbox' of thinking skills – a toolbox they can dip into at the most appropriate moments. Mark Creasy reminds us that it doesn't mean we don't teach the basic skills of literacy and numeracy, but that we can choose skills-driven methods to allow children to see the different ways there might be to learning things.

Sarah Noble, head of department, modern foreign languages

With this book, Mark Creasy has tackled an area of education (homework) which has long needed addressing. As a Year 4 teacher, I can readily connect with his ideas and the thinking behind *Unhomework*. I am sure that other teachers will do the same.

The book's informal style makes it enjoyable to read whilst dealing with what can sometimes be a 'touchy' subject between teachers, children and parents.

Mark has used some catchy chapter headings to engage the reader and in each chapter he 'says it how it is', in real-life situations. Interspersed with the theory are snippets of Mark's humour and wit. Each chapter leads effortlessly on to the next.

Not only will this book appeal to teachers but it will also interest parents. As I am sure Mark will agree, when it comes to homework, getting parents on board is half the battle.

Davina Suggett, Year 4 teacher

Mark Creasy expertly steers you away from the trials and tribulations of homework and into the realms of Unhomework! This book is not just about making the most of lost opportunities for additional learning; it really gets to grips with how and why children learn and how the traditional concept of homework does not necessarily do what it is supposed to. As a teacher or school leader there is much to consider here. Be prepared to read this book, reflect on your own experiences of homework, be convinced there is a better way of doing things and then go to school and make some changes!

Allow Mark to help you with ideas and inspiration for making a difference to your children's learning. Allow him to inspire whole school policy on learning and explore the true benefits of Unhomework. When you read this book, and you should, you will see how important it is to make the most of learning opportunities in school and at home.

As a parent, I often get frustrated with the standard and relevance of the homework my own children receive. Maybe at the next parents' evening I should casually leave a copy of *Unhomework* on the desk and see what transpires!

Unhomework will give you the inspiration and practical guidance you need to break free from the 'curse of the worksheet'.

Dave Whitaker, executive principal, Springwell Community Special School and Barnsley PRU

Unhomework is an interesting concept and one which may strike fear into a few colleagues who cling on to the security blanket of the worksheet-style approach to homework – after all, it is a rare constant in this ever-changing educational landscape! At a time when a new curriculum is being introduced, this book suggests how we may grasp the chance to try something new and 'dovetail' it into a creative approach to all that we do in school. This is a golden opportunity to truly let pupils lead their own learning and follow trails of enquiry that will motivate and engage them. Not only that, it will also increase the chances of getting parents on board. This is a book with plenty of ideas for teachers and practical ways for parents to support their children.

Beverley Dandy, head teacher, Outwoods Primary School

Whenever I run a parents' session about homework, the results are almost always the same. Some parents believe that schools should be chastised for setting second-rate homework, such as 'finish off what you were doing in class' or, just as bad, MOTS (more of the same) and so miss an opportunity to stimulate additional learning in their children. On the other hand, some parents question the value and purpose of homework as a substitute for the many exciting things they could be doing with their family instead. Still others believe the school is trying to turn them into teachers, at best, or dictators, at worst, who police the quality and quantity of their child's homework. For any child caught in the middle, this can be extremely frustrating, but for a highly able child it can be nothing short of torture. Imagine having all those ideas going round in your head and being told to do something far more boring and meaningless! I was therefore delighted when I was asked to read and review Mark's book about Unhomework. The structure it suggests for challenging children so that they go as far as their potential allows is so interesting that I would recommend it to every teacher and challenge them, whether they are in primary or secondary school, to implement it for just one term and evaluate the results. I will certainly be including references to his approach in our future workshops on homework.

Denise Yates, chief executive, Potential plus UK (formerly the National Association for Gifted Children)

UNHOMEWORK

HOW TO GET THE MOST OUT OF HOMEWORK WITHOUT REALLY SETTING IT

MARK CREASY

Independent Thinking Press

First published by

Independent Thinking Press
Crown Buildings, Bancyfelin, Carmarthen, Wales, SA33 5ND, UK
www.independentthinkingpress.com
Independent Thinking Press is an imprint of Crown House Publishing Ltd.

First published 2014. Reprinted 2014.

British Library Cataloguing-in-Publication Data

A catalogue entry for this book is available from the British Library.

Print ISBN 978-178135109-3
Mobi ISBN 978-178135154-3
ePub ISBN 978-178135155-0
ePDF ISBN 978-178135156-7

Edited by Peter Young

Printed and bound in the UK by
Gomer Press, Llandysul, Ceredigion

For Deryn, Jessica and Thomas, thank you for your inspiration

ACKNOWLEDGEMENTS

This book wouldn't have been possible were it not for a huge cast of people. Firstly, Deryn and Jessica, you are the reason I do everything I do. You inspire me every day to try to be better than I was the day before; thank you for your love, support and unstinting encouragement. Also, to my mum and dad, who'd have thought a council estate boy from Hayes (correctly pronounced 'ayes) would have a book? Thanks to you I do!

I can't name every colleague I've ever worked with, but I have to give special thanks to Daryll, Shirley and Rhett – you made such an impact at the key times in my professional career – and to Andrew B for your encouragement and guidance when I needed it most. Similarly, it's impossible to list every child I have ever taught who has inspired, challenged, provoked, spurred and taught me, but this book is for you all and those who follow.

Finally a huge thank you to Ian Gilbert, Caroline Lenton and Peter Young for seeing potential in the idea of 'Unhomework' and supporting me through the entire process; without you the book wouldn't have been written. To anyone else who thinks they should have been mentioned, I apologise; it wasn't done on purpose – well, probably not!

CONTENTS

INTRODUCTION

This book began life as an idea that grew out of a chance conversation and follow-up email discussion with Ian Gilbert following the Independent Thinking 'Big Day Out' in Nottingham. Two years later, this book is the expression of over ten years' practical work in classrooms across four schools. During this time I have achieved the position of head teacher and have taught a range of subjects to children from Year 4 to Year 13. This will hopefully continue for a long time to come.

I qualified as a physical education teacher at Exeter in the late 1990s. Then, as now, PE didn't require homework as such, so in the earlier days of my teaching career I didn't need to worry about it. However, as I moved away from the gym and into the classroom, initially teaching my second subject of English, I realised more and more that homework was pretty much a waste of time – not just the children's time, but the teacher's time as well. Apart from the hours, effort and paper which went into such work, most of the homework I set until that time simply confirmed what I already knew: that it didn't really take the children any further or deeper into their understanding. It was just homework for homework's sake. I have to admit that I just copied the pattern I saw colleagues using, arguing that I was simply 'following the scheme'. But this was not how I taught. Simply following a lesson scheme wasn't how I worked inside the classroom and it wasn't how I wanted my classes to perform outside of it either. Yes, I was one of those (annoying) colleagues who could set the work and the children would bring it in, which was something that my homework-chasing colleagues would often complain about. They either had to ask repeatedly, or they didn't get it in at all.

I couldn't help thinking that traditional homework was putting us on some sort of educational hamster's wheel. I used to put a lot of time and effort into preparing the copies of the work for each child, which they went away and completed for me to mark, but neither of us were really enjoying the process. This kind of learning was neither exciting nor rewarding – for me or for them. However, as a 'maverick in the classroom' (as one of my head teachers put it), following the same ritual as everyone else didn't sit comfortably. I spoke to other colleagues, but at that time none of us felt empowered enough to challenge the status quo, and sadly, as the children expected or knew no different, so it continued.

Ironically, given the perspective some people have about certain types of schools, it was when I was working in a Special Measures school in Luton in 2003 that my homework epiphany came. Although many people believe Special Measures to be constraining and about box ticking, one of the wonderful things about Special Measures is the freedom it gives you if you're prepared to take it. The clue is in the name: you're working together on doing something different, because whatever it was before, it didn't work. It was Dale who was instrumental in my change of mind. Dale, a Year 10 boy, would have been described as a loveable rogue by those who knew him. The middle child of a large family, he had the charm and smile to compensate for his usual lack of work and effort and was one of those children whom you just wished would recognise how talented he really was. However, football and girls were more his focus! I was teaching him GCSE English when he burst one of the great educational myths. He said, 'So, I have to spend at least an hour every night doing my homework, yet I'm supposed to be developing myself into a rounded young man – whatever that means.' He continued, 'Then, you spend even longer marking it all. But you have a family you must want to be with. Surely there's a better way than all this, isn't there? Why do we both put ourselves through this, when we could be doing other, more enjoyable and fun things instead?'

I thought about what he'd said and realised that Dale was right: it was time to break the pattern. There really was no point to homework; well, certainly not in the ritualistic way in which I had been setting it up to then. In fact, for the first time ever I began to look at the very nature of homework in a more holistic manner, in terms of how it was getting in the way of having a good life for me and my classes. This was with special regard to the buzz phrase 'lifelong learning' with which I was being bombarded at work, in the TES and at every course I went on at that time. I had to reconsider whether I was truly doing my bit to ensure and cement this philosophy. I came to the conclusion that, unfortunately and somewhat depressingly, I wasn't. It was at that moment that I resolved to do something different. However, despite my personal revelation, I worked in a school with a clear homework policy and expectations.

It was from this discussion with Dale – coupled with the need to be able to provide evidence that my children did 'complete homework' – that the idea of 'Unhomework' began to form in my mind. I had never given what I did a proper name, always referring to how I set homework as 'not really doing it' or 'getting homework in without setting it'. However, these aren't catchy names, nor do they sum up the essence of what I have learned to do as a classroom teacher over the past decade, so I now use the term coined by Ian Gilbert – Unhomework.

During this time Unhomework has become an integral part of my educational philosophy and an ingrained process for ensuring that my children – regardless of the age or phase I was teaching – completed work outside of the classroom which was relevant, purposeful and engaging for them, as well as being aligned with the ideals they encounter within the classroom. Unhomework allows the children to lead their learning, as I encourage them to do in the class. My aim is to achieve the position of the 'guide at the side'. In this role, I find they need me less and less as the year progresses.

As you might expect, the Unhomework idea did not come fully formed, but developed gradually, with plenty of learning from my experience of working with over 1,500 children in the classroom. I have benefited greatly from the comments made by my colleagues, the parents and, more importantly, the children who have passed through my classes during the last decade who were tolerant of the mistakes and explorations I was making along the way. In retrospect, I can see now that I was providing them with a good role model for getting on in life.

These days, Unhomework is an essential part of my entire classroom experience. The model I have developed builds on the creative curriculum and project-based learning ideals of establishing an enquiry within a context. From this, the children then develop and answer their enquiries, before elaborating them as they decide appropriate, creating greater breadth, depth or both, or even opening up a new enquiry sparked by their learning. In this way, children are freed from the shackles of being set standardised homework. Unhomework provides greater autonomy for them and, when done properly, eases the teacher's burden too.

I estimate that I have now used this approach with well over 1,500 children personally, as well as indirectly with countless others, thanks to colleagues adopting the practice. This autumn I have just introduced another class of children to Unhomework. As I currently work in primary education, I have come to realise that this process is best begun there, as it allows children to grow and develop with it as they progress through education.

To answer some recent government criticisms, specifically from Civil Society Minister Nick Hurd: it helps develop 'grit, resilience and independence' in their learning – though it was doing this long before it was today's stick to beat schools with. I can honestly say that it works for children at any age and it doesn't detract from exams or from anything else. On the contrary, it enhances them, and when introduced and explained properly, it does provide them – as Dale challenged me all that time ago – with opportunities to become more rounded human beings.

CHAPTER ONE
UNHOMEWORK VS HOMEWORK

Homework

Benjamin Franklin famously said, 'Tell me and I forget, teach me and I may remember, involve me and I learn.' In my experience, and from the feedback of children I have spoken to during my teaching career across six schools, this is not how children view homework. Unfortunately, the following scene is more common:

The bell rings.

Teacher (*over the shuffling of feet and scraping of chairs*): Right, I want you to get down today's homework.

Class: (*Collective groaning, some not even bothering to get homework diaries out … again*)

Teacher: It's not my fault; you know it's the rule!

Class: (*Groaning louder*)

Teacher: Right, it's there on the board. I want it in next lesson.

The class's next lesson.

Teacher: Where's your homework?

Child: What homework?

Teacher: The one I set at the end of last lesson.

Child: I forgot to write it down as I needed the loo before next class.

Teacher: Well get it to me tomorrow then. (*To another child*) What about yours, why is it in that state?

Child: I've done it!

Teacher: But it's not what you're capable of, is it?

Child: But I did it – isn't it good enough?

Teacher (*in desperation, grateful it's been done and realising time is ebbing from the lesson*): Of course, it's just I'd like it to be neater to show more care and pride.

Child (*walking off, muttering*): Maybe you show the same and don't set it in two minutes, after the bell.

This scene was the reality for a Year 10 geography class I was in the process of observing for peer support of the teacher. It hit at the very crux of the homework dilemma: we set what parents, peers and children expect. It also hit at the heart of the teacher's issues too: time management and trying to do everything, without giving the children ownership of their learning – but that is another story.

An alternative problem also derives from the best practice of many teachers, advocated in all six of the schools in which I have worked: setting the homework at the start of the lesson. Here are two exchanges from different classes, one recounted from a child's perspective and another I observed, which show how this can also be fraught with problems:

My conversation

I was mentoring Year 11 students, trying to raise aspirations and make some of them realise how able they were, as well as delivering a swift kick up the backside for others! As Jake sat down I smiled inwardly. For the past three years he had been able to get to the heart of pretty much any issue in the school; in fact the head would often ask why the senior leadership team (SLT) was required when all we needed to do was to leave Jake in charge! Essentially, he was the school's Huggy Bear. If you wanted 'the word on the street', Jake knew it, intimately! Always able to dance on the right side of the school rules, he was a loveable rogue who used charm where his ability failed him. He was already being spoken of by some of us as a potential head boy in the sixth form – much to the amazement of others, who had not encountered Jake in full flow!

After looking at target grades, progress and what Jake expected to do after Year 11 the conversation, as was scripted, turned to the section 'How can the school help me more in my learning?' This was the bit I knew would prove enlightening, though I was concerned whether the half-side of A4 box I had would be enough! I posed the question and waited …

Jake (*shifting in his seat, looking at me seriously*): Mr Creasy, it's simple.

MC: Really?

Jake: Yeah, I reckon it could be solved in three, maybe four simple ways.

MC: You've thought about this Jake, so what are they?

Jake: You might not like the answers, you know.

MC: If I wanted only answers I liked I wouldn't ask!

Jake: Okay, hmm, where to start … Okay …

Jake then led me on a critical analysis of what needed to be done, starting with the simple, 'If you want children to behave better, get the teachers to be on time and meet us at the door with a smile, not bark down the corridor, or from inside the room shout "In" because *they're* late.' He provided more detailed analyses of lessons, commenting on pace, variety and learning styles: 'Why can't I use my art skills in more lessons? I could make notes in pictures. Shouldn't it be *my* decision how I want *my* revision notes to look, not the teachers?'

Until finally he said, 'The last thing, er, how many is that now?' After hearing this was point nine of the original three or four he smiled:

Jake: Homework.

MC: Homework?

Jake: Yep. Now I'm giving away some serious secrets here, but I trust you!

MC (*laughing inwardly at his naivety*): Thank you!

Jake: Well, you know the school is divided into three groups of teachers, well four, but one group is split in two.

MC: I didn't, Jake, how so?

Jake (*without pride or bravado, just matter of fact*): Well, first, since Year 9 I've pretty much done no homework, you know.

MC: What? Now I know that's not true, I teach you.

Jake: Well, you don't count really.

MC: Thanks!

Jake: Don't take offence, it's a compliment!

MC: Hmm, we differ on compliments then!

Jake (*smiling*): Let me explain, then you'll see! The first group are the late setters, you know the ones, bell rings and they've forgotten to set it 'cos they've focused on the starter, main and dessert.

MC: Plenary.

Jake: Whatever! Well it's easy. I always sit at the front, so for them I say I didn't copy it down as I had left the room. They believe me! So I don't do their work and if they think to ask me to do it the following week, we discuss if it's fair for me to do double and agree it's not!

MC: Okay, the second group?

Jake: Oh, they're even better! They set theirs at the start of the lesson and this is the two part group. The first of these is to complete the worksheet. Somehow I always lose it, forget it or something else. Or if it's a look-it-up-on-the-Internet, my computer is broken – it never is though!

MC: Okay, what about the second part of that group?

Jake: Oh, them? They're my favourite! They set it at the start, telling us that we'll understand it by the end of the lesson. I start off by interrogating the sheet with all the 'how, what, where' questions I can. Then, at the end of the lesson, when they're doing that plenary thing, I can go through what I don't understand about the lesson and how I can't do the homework.

MC: But surely they offer to help you out?

Jake: They do, but that's the beauty of it. I ask them why I'm being punished for not understanding the lesson and have to give up my time to do the homework. That always throws them! They get all flustered and say they'll give me some help next lesson and not to worry about the homework.

MC: Very clever!

Jake: And actually most staff just think 'Oh, it's Jake' and don't even worry about my homework.

MC: Perhaps that explains some of your grades?

Jake: Harsh!

MC: But fair! So what about the final group then?

Jake: Oh, that's easy, it's you!

MC: Me?

Jake: Yeah, the way you set homework, making us think for ourselves and making us responsible, you make me not want to let myself down and if I don't do it it's my fault! That's sneaky!

MC: Ah, now I see why it was a compliment earlier.

Jake: Yeah, just don't tell the other teachers – you're the only one I do homework for.

MC: No Jake, *you're* the only one you do homework for!

Jake (*grinning*): Fair enough, you got me there!

When the mentoring was fed back to staff, Jake's comments were highlighted. Some staff were shocked, but for others it helped them to look into changing their way of setting homework so that Jake was soon doing more homework than just for me!

My observation

Class enters, sits down and gets on with the starter activity. All good so far. They have clear routines and set expectations, and follow them. The teacher then directs the children to the freshly powered-up PowerPoint which has the homework on, which they duly copy into homework planners as the teacher hands out the sheet they are to complete. The instructions say: 'Fill in the sheet below, highlighting any answers that you had to look up.' It is due the next lesson. The task is a cloze exercise and there are three different types of sheet being handed out, so on the surface differentiation is being covered.

After the lesson, which went well, with the children making good progress, the teacher outlined her frustration about the homework. She knew it was better practice to set it at the start of a lesson, but then, so that she didn't miss covering what the children needed for completing the work, she would have to set prosaic work, or review previous learning or set up future tasks. Any of these, whilst providing summative or formative assessment, might also put some children off. In the case of reviewing work, trying to maintain true differentiation for the entire class to meet all of their needs was a practical impossibility. This had led to the cursory three-tiered approach to differentiation I had witnessed in the observation. As for setting work yet to be undertaken, the colleague had found that many children panicked with things they had not encountered in class. This led to the homework taking too long and causing parental complaints or to it not being done at all as children felt like failures, or becoming a self-fulfilling prophecy when the lessons on that topic began. Instead of being a true reflection or baseline of the children's ability, the opposite was true with her homework. Here was a colleague, somebody liked and respected by staff, parents and children alike, who was feeling bowed by the expectations of homework. We discussed her thoughts and I explained how Unhomework worked – she knew it would make a real difference.

What is the problem with homework?

There is increasing research evidence which supports my long-held view that there is no point to the traditional form of homework. I have become increasingly frustrated with the inadequacies of the traditional homework system, and have made numerous small changes in the way I allocate homework in the classes of children I have been teaching; however, my Unhomework approach is still developing, given all the input I receive from colleagues, children and parents. Unhomework is designed to address all of the points above, as outlined in my conversation with Jake and the scenarios at the start of the chapter. It has shown itself to be of greater benefit than traditional, routine and formulaic homework in that it truly meets the needs of children's learning.

Whilst parents, teachers, lecturers, employers and ministers may disagree on the form of education children should receive and the requisite skills they should possess when they leave school, the common ground appears to be the necessity for employability skills. Therefore, the myth about homework being 'life preparation' is over-simplistic; we need a twenty-first-century workforce to cope with the technological, social, moral and philosophical challenges we face (for further reading on this subject, see Thomas L Friedman's *The World is Flat*).

Even the word homework is unhelpful, given the wide number of tasks it encompasses. Here is a sample from the past two weeks at my current school for Year 5 and 6 children:

+ Memorise (the French alphabet and spellings)

+ Answer (maths booklet)

+ Research (a wife of Henry VIII)

+ Read (to the end of a chapter for English)

+ Write (a factfile for a famous scientist)

+ Create (a model of the water cycle)

+ Complete (the sentences using synonyms)

+ Match (words to their synonyms)

+ Interview (someone about recycling)

This list is clearly not exhaustive. It says nothing of discussing, drawing, baking (yes, baking!), viewing, listening or other tasks which I have not included here. Therefore, the issues are:

+ No teacher can be reasonably expected to provide quality, differentiated homework for their entire class – certainly not each and every week (and if they do, they need to get a reality check on what the children are learning).

+ Not all parents are experts in every subject, nor are they able to assist their child adequately or match the current teaching methodology. Instead, they may only have their own school experience to base things on, and that may not have been a good one!

+ Teachers should be focusing on making learning inspiring and engaging, and treating homework as an essential part of the learning process.

+ Children need some time to develop their own pursuits and interests, which will make them well-rounded, rather than spending all their free time within the confines of academic education.

+ Traditionally set homework does not inspire lifelong independent learning; it is more often a tick box assignment (and then forgotten).

+ Children know well enough what they are capable of and should be taught to address this for themselves.

+ Children should be given the opportunity to demonstrate their talents and present their work in a way that engages them and creates interest in others.

And then comes the battle over completing inane, uninspiring, insipid homework. In many cases, all it does is provide succour to the question raised in the title of Ian Gilbert's *Why Do I Need a Teacher When I've Got Google?*, as this is the destination for many homework tasks. Staff may set a task to meet the expectations I have spoken of but it will not really develop the children as they can simply access Google and find the answer. Need to research Henry VIII? Google will give you reams of information. Want to know about recycling in your area? Google searches will give you text and charts for this. Need a factfile on a famous scientist? A Google search, probably via Wikipedia, will provide more information than you need – or can understand if you're in Year 5 or 6! As Ian Gilbert points out in his book, it's not just about fact learning and memorising, but about inspiring and instilling a love of the subject, which traditionally set homework doesn't lend itself to. I am not blaming the teachers for setting such homework, it's just that this process has become a rather hackneyed game being played out in classrooms all over the country. What saddens me is that they haven't thought of, or had time to think of, an alternative.

The homework game is played according to some or all of the following 'rules':

1   The teacher sets the homework – preferably at the start of the lesson so the children can write it down in time.

2   The child completes it during the intervening period before the next class, with or without help from colleagues, parents and so on. Their output is differentiated from other pupils by their ability to complete the task at hand (or rather, whether or not they can copy and paste adequately, or whether they use their own words for what they've read online).

3   They hand it in, or the teacher chases them to get it, or punishes them for not handing it in.

4   The teacher marks it using some kind of intellectual template, where evaluation appears in the form of stock phrases and clichés, given they've all used only the first or second website from their Google search list.

5   The teacher hands it back.

6   The child only looks at the mark or grade.

7   The teacher encourages the child to read the comments.

8   There is no adequate use of the feedback, as neither you nor the child have allocated quality time to do anything with the comments because the curriculum demands we need to move on to the next theme/topic. So we return to stage 1, but we congratulate ourselves that we have met/obeyed the school homework (and marking) policy.

That is not to say that some teacher colleagues do not try hard to resist this and develop a more creative approach. I know many do, but too many fall prey to this hamster-wheel existence, if only to get by.

This is where family life can potentially break down. Parents, wanting the best for their children, support, encourage or enforce the doing of homework at the expense of enjoying quality time with their child. It may escalate into the nightly battle many friends describe to me. They may even agree with their child's complaints about its pointlessness, but as this fits the model they were exposed to at school, it makes sense to continue with it as, by and large, it didn't do them any harm. Hence, their time to cherish and nurture their child is dissipated and they are dragged onto a similar hamster wheel to the teacher, but do so whilst juggling their own work, home and family requirements, as well as trying to find time for themselves. And none of this provides any benefit for the children.

I have witnessed this first-hand and have had it recounted by colleagues across Britain. In France, homework is banned in primary schools – it has been since 1956, though recently French parents felt the need for action as teachers were ignoring this legislation and sending tasks home. In fact, the Fédération des Conseils de Parents d'Elèves (FCPE – the French Parents' association, with representatives in almost all French schools) has led a nationwide boycott of *devoirs* (homework exercises), which 'put pressure on children' and cause a burden to their parents who 'do not have sufficient knowledge' to help their children. However, I am not for a moment arguing for a move towards the French system. Unhomework offers a different approach and actually allows children to develop themselves, at the same time providing parents with opportunities to support them properly and enjoy the feeling of fulfilment and purpose when they do.

One simplistic solution to the routine homework problem would be to treat all the teachers setting such homework in a similar manner – not as individuals, but part of a homogeneous mass with no consideration of their individual needs. Just imagine the response in a staffroom to that! In fact, forget imagining it – think back to the most recent poor INSET you've received. You know the type: all staff, irrespective of role/responsibility/experience/interest, get the same delivery – invariably PowerPoint being read to you! Now, how did you like that? Were you excited, thinking, 'Wow! I can't wait to try that out!' or were you more along the lines of, 'That's *x* minutes of my life I'll never get back'? Now ask yourself: why don't my children deserve what I expect? What's stopping me from giving them a better deal? So, towards this end, I want to be supportive and offer solutions to the problem. What Unhomework can deliver, which traditionally set homework cannot, is individuality and purpose for every child, whilst not expecting miracles from teachers to achieve it.

The curse of the worksheet

Something similar needs to happen to work-sheet-based homework, which could be any of the following: fill in the blanks, complete a crossword, do a word search or tick the box exercises. Or, the most demeaning, colouring in. All of these are clearly designed to say, 'I've set the homework as the policy states (but I can't be arsed to make it meaningful!).'

I am not saying that these kinds of activities are inappropriate for younger children. I know from Key Stage 1 and Foundation Stage colleagues that there can be some merit in these approaches. For example, supporting the weaker speller with multiple choice options of words can prevent demotivation and underpin their knowledge of how words are used correctly. Similarly, I have seen my own daughter, who has struggled with times tables, enjoy a colouring exercise where all of the numbers from a specific table created a picture, thus showing differentiation and recognising that she is a creative girl and that a bare sheet of sums would not engage her. However, from personal experience in observing my colleagues and as a parent, I too often feel that the homework set only serves to prove John Abbott's observation: 'Teachers do what they believe in extraordinarily well, but what they are told to do merely to a mediocre standard.'[1]

Perhaps the greatest irony is the use of worksheet homework for topics such as 'The Rainforest' or 'The Environment', where children are taught about deforestation, yet still we cut down trees and waste paper

---

1   http://www.21learn.org/uncategorized/the-making-of-teachers/

in setting homework! This can then be compounded when the child researches the work on Wikipedia and, as they have not been taught to do otherwise, or maybe as they're at home without a limit, they print the entire webpage to hand in. After all, why copy and paste, let alone read and rewrite, when you can simply click 'Print' to show how much research you have done? That is not to blame the child; in my opinion, some blame must be apportioned to the teacher for setting work that can be answered in this way and/or not teaching correct website researching. The child will reason out the following:

+ What have I got to do?

+ What else do I want to be doing?

+ Which is my preference?

+ What is my maximum output for my minimum input?

+ Can I get away with this and leave myself with more time for friends, sport, clubs, gaming, music, shopping, etc.?

If the answer to the last point is 'yes' then the system breaks down. This is especially true, given how many parents are relieved to hear those magic words, 'I've already done my homework.' This eases their burden and the need to take to the battleground. Now they can choose to believe (however vaguely) that this is one thing they can tick off their list after their hard day at work.

Ironically, the government appears to be in (partial) agreement with this standpoint on the futility of setting homework simply because we have to. Michael Gove announced in March 2012 that there would now be no government guidelines about how much homework a child should do each night and that this, instead, should fall to individual head teachers.[2] This was a clear change from the previous expectations of an hour a week for five- to seven-year-olds, building to 2.5 hours for up to sixteen-year-olds.[3] I'm sure that head teachers will like this, for, as we know,

---

2   http://www.telegraph.co.uk/education/9121048/Michael-Gove-scraps-homework-rules.html

3   http://www.bbc.co.uk/newsround/17255075

they clearly have nothing better to do (especially in the current education climate). From now on it will be much easier, thanks to the direction the new curriculum appears to be taking: all homework needs to be fact-based rather than stimulating!

The Department of Education claims that this decision apparently came as the result of parental comments and complaints about their child's lack of time to do sports and other activities and their need to spend time with their families. Although Michael Gove may be frequently criticised for failing to listen to the views of others, especially when contrary to his own, I hope this decision will be carried out, given that in the same month 70% of responders to an online *Guardian* survey believed children get too much homework.

What is Unhomework?

Unhomework is a philosophy and process for ensuring that the work your class completes outside of the classroom is relevant, purposeful and engaging for them, whatever their age or phase of education. I established it to extend the way in which I work with the children in my class into the way they can work in their own time. My aim was to allow them to develop those attributes and enhance their learning through self-motivation. Furthermore, it was designed to allow them to recognise and show off their strengths, rather than just meeting the requirements of the work which had been set. If done properly, under conditions that allow it to flourish, Unhomework will support children in addressing their areas for development too, giving them the confidence and security to try different things.

Unhomework can be defined as 'homework without really setting it'. It is work that the children are inspired to complete without being told to. This is because it relates to their learning and empowers them to confirm their understanding by taking the lesson further or in a different direction, or, better still, by applying it in their own way. The children actually state upfront what they intend to do (unless they decide to take on an exploratory 'mission') and then produce the evidence of their endeavours in the given time. The children will agree the timeframe for completion with the teacher, based on what it is they are going to produce, and they will also state the criteria against which it will be marked, usually with due reference to Bloom's Taxonomy. So the evidence will demonstrate knowledge or understanding, analysis, application or evaluation, or even synthesise the learning. From this, the evidence (which is presented in any appropriate form, decided by the child) is shared with the class, then self- and peer-assessed against the criteria, before being checked by the teacher. Once this process has occurred, or even during it as discussions abound about what each child is doing, the work can be built on by the individual. This can be done for either depth or breadth of study, not only for the child whose work it is, but for the whole class, as they are inspired by their peers.

This concept builds on the ideals of the Personal, Learning and Thinking Skills (PLTS – see Appendix 1) in striving to support the children in becoming:

+ Creative thinkers

+ Reflective learners

+ Team workers

+ Independent enquirers

+ Effective participators

+ Self-managers

To me, these are essential attributes for learners to develop, and they go hand in hand with the Qualifications and Curriculum Authority's (QCA) Big Picture[4] which despite unfortunately falling out of

---

[4] http://webarchive.nationalarchives.gov.uk/20080806121643/
http://qca.org.uk/libraryAssets/media/Big_Picture_2008.pdf

favour with the coalition government, provided the three excellent fundamentals of the curriculum, supporting children in becoming:

+ Successful learners

+ Confident individuals

+ Responsible citizens

The QCA wanted to ensure that the curriculum children were to receive supported these ideals, and believed that everything flowed from there. This seems a perfectly reasonable aim, because who wouldn't want their child or class to achieve this? I have also found that when I introduce how I want to work with a class and what my aspirations are for them, these six simple words sum it all up. The PLTS are there to amplify them and Unhomework thus becomes easier to comprehend, as it is not clear how children can really become self-managing creative thinkers if we simply prescribe routine homework. How can they become reflective learners if the homework they complete is never developed further?

Therefore, Unhomework finds natural support from the creative curriculum, enquiry-based learning and project-based learning. It is designed to free the children from the straitjacket of standardised homework. Unhomework allows the children greater autonomy and, in addition, eases the teachers' burdens. However, this is not a simple rebranding job. Unhomework relies on being properly introduced and appropriately modelled for the children's understanding, ensuring that the children fully realise the extent of the freedom they are being given – alongside the responsibility this brings.

HOW TO SECURE UNHOMEWORK IN YOUR CLASSROOM

Creating a climate for Unhomework

Unhomework is both a philosophy and a process. It doesn't happen by deciding not to set homework, but by you actively choosing to do homework using the process outlined here. Underpinning this process is the belief that it needs to be done in a different way. I know from colleagues that this is not a belief universally held. However, once you have experienced the difference with the children, you will need to start changing the classroom learning itself.

Essentially, it has to be about securing firm foundations for learning. Without the right climate for every child, learning will be impeded, both inside and then outside of the classroom. How can you hope to establish a new style of homework if you carry on the same way in the class, or if you do not already have the environment which will breed the ideas?

When I first began to consider challenging the status quo, I hit upon an idea which I call the 5Rs, which I still use to underpin my children's learning. They are:

+ Respect

+ Relationships

+ Resilience

+ Responsibilities

+ Rights

I see these 5Rs as the most significant elements for securing the Unhomework philosophy and practice in the children I teach.

In subsequent years I have used these to build upon the PLTS which permeate our work both inside and outside the class. They become part of the daily vocabulary my class are exposed to from the moment I meet them in September, and are soon incorporated into their learning. All of the 5Rs are interrelated and dependent upon each other. Whenever I detect that things are not as I would like in my classroom, I unfailingly find a deficiency in one particular area, which is then causing a domino effect on the other areas.

Having five to remember makes it easier for the children to recall by counting them off on their fingers. As the American philosopher and educator Mortimer Adler said,

The purpose of learning is growth, and our minds, unlike our bodies, can continue growing as we continue to live.

The more I have worked using the 5Rs, the more I have come to appreciate how important it is to get them right from the off. I work on them in the order I have listed them. I am also aware that other colleagues may want to consider or highlight other 'Rs'; as with Howard Gardner's multiple intelligences, if these five do no more than prompt discussion and lead to greater understanding, and even development, then I'll be delighted.

Each of my 5Rs could be expanded into a book in its own right, but here is a brief outline of the reasons and ideas behind each one, as well as some ways to secure them.

Respect

This is respect for themselves, for each other, for their teachers and for their environment. Unfortunately, these are too often seen as ideals and only paid lip service. First, we need to address the question: how can we hope to instil respect for anyone or anything, if at first we do not support children to respect their own being?

One of the saddest experiences in my career was with one little girl, who upon finding out that I was to be her teacher exclaimed, 'Finally, a teacher who likes me!' It doesn't matter whether that was actually the case, but to her it was true; her perception was her reality. From that day I worked to ensure she never doubted that I liked her – however hard she made it! As Ian Gilbert says, 'Teaching is a four-letter word – love.'

Unfortunately, we work in a country where the phrase 'too clever for his/her own good' is still uttered (although 'too clever for my lesson plan' is probably more accurate!). This phrase is not exactly a firm foundation for building a child's self-respect. If we want a child to respect themself then we need to encourage and build in them a recognition of their strengths and areas for development. Children need to have their successes celebrated and shouted from the rooftops, and they also need to be supported at times when they are too embarrassed or insecure to recognise these things for themselves.

At this point there'll be colleagues flexing their typing fingers to point out, 'But what about their areas for development?' Or even to ask, 'But if you do this, then what about those that can't do it?' Funnily enough, in my experience, they can cope with this recognition, and Unhomework helps them. I learned this early on when I was studying at Exeter University. I had been fortunate enough to be invited on a primary visit with the late, great Professor Ted Wragg (he was my PGCE tutor). As we were sitting at a table one child asked us, 'Can you spell "because"?' After considering how to help the child spell it for himself, but unsure of the school policy for spelling, we both decided to simply confirm we could spell 'because', to which we were told, 'Then you're on the wrong table; we can't spell "because" on here, you need to be over there.'

A treasured memory from my time as a primary teacher shows this ethos at work in my classroom. One of the weakest spellers in my class got 8/10 in a test, and this led to the entire class bursting into spontaneous applause at such an achievement for this child. Remarkably, not one of the eleven children who had got 10/10 was jealous or surly, or pointed out their own achievement, or even that this child had easier spellings. Why? I believe they had received respect from me on a daily basis so they were able to respect themselves as complete individuals, and this made it easier to have respect for each other, knowing that this was the basis for our class.

Establishing Respect in preparation for Unhomework:

+ Most importantly, get to know them, find out what they do and what they are good at, both inside and outside of school. The English teacher who can congratulate the footballer or the maths teacher congratulating the dancer for recent performances is so empowering.

+ Recognise successes. Have a 'Wall of Fame', to which you and the children contribute, to highlight and reinforce what you are celebrating.

+ Show and tell. This is a great device in primary classrooms which can also work in secondary, just on a different level.

◆ 'When I was at primary school …' Get secondary children to share primary school experiences: what did they enjoy? What were their significant 'learnings'? Get them to revisit those times with older, wiser heads.

◆ Play 'I wish I was you'. This is a really simple game, which is exactly as its name suggests. It can be done verbally, by passing sticky notes, or on paper dropped in a box. Whatever way you play it, from an anonymous postbox to open verbal discussion, the children state who they wish they were in the class and why. With the correct trust in the room this is tremendously empowering and almost always provides an instant response from the recipient about an attribute they admire in the compliment provider.

◆ Hold discussions where children listen to each other and learn to appreciate other points of view – even if they disagree with them.

Relationships

By respecting themselves and others, the children recognise that they are part of a group and use collaboration to support and develop themselves, not only with their teacher(s), but with their peers. In the brand/brave new world of globalised learning that today's children will enter as adolescents and adults, the need to work with others is fundamental. The video 'Shift Happens' has demonstrated this for numerous years now.[1] This is in alignment with the PLTS principles. If our children are to be prepared for such an environment, these peers need to extend beyond their immediate friendship group to those they would not usually select to partner or group with.

In more enlightened schools, this respect also extends across year groups and key stages – even sectors. It is more than just paying lip service to the notion; it's about actively becoming proponents of

---

[1] http://www.youtube.com/watch?v=FdTOFkhaplo

this 'cross-fertilised' way of working. (Remember, it is only in schools that are we grouped by our age, irrespective of need. This says a lot about how we view the young people entrusted into our care every day!)

From what I have picked up from discussions with colleagues, in far too many classrooms across our country children are not taught reliance on others, or even the need to value and trust their peers. It is in this determination to fulfil the mantle of personalisation that we discover the isolation of the learner, their over-reliance on themselves and a complete lack of confidence in others. This is not to say that I am against personalisation, not at all. It's rather that too often children do not receive true personalisation and bespoke education. Instead, it is more a case of sweepingly generalised work which is tweaked for certain groups of children within the class (frequently to meet a set of data points required for whole school analysis). This obviously does not achieve truly individualised work.

Phil Beadle points out in his books (refer to the bibliography for a list) that children love group work and want to work together. They know this is how they learn best and want to do so more often. And forget that prescriptive and formulaic mantra that boys only want competition and girls only want collaboration. That is over-simplistic, a false dichotomy, because it ignores the fact that we all need both to some degree, at different times. Members of my previous classes will testify that girls love competition too, especially if it involves beating the boys! PLTS cover this easily, showing aspects for self and team and how each is blended – occasionally recognising this can be the sole purpose of an activity in class.

This is best exemplified by the time when the three children in my class who were strongest at English failed to work together effectively to analyse a poem, becoming increasingly frustrated that 'weaker' classmates could do it. By referring them back to the PLTS, rather than the task itself, they recognised where they had gone wrong.

The 'weaker' group had understood how to be effective team workers and participators from the PLTS, and by ensuring that those attributes were being used, it allowed them to work harmoniously, to each have a role in analysing the poem. The three strongest children were too busy shouting each other down, trying to lead and finding their own gems to show off their knowledge to meet the task. In fact, they had all asked me if they could work by themselves! But, by referring them back to the PLTS, they had to plan how they could do things differently next time. At the end of the year they all remembered this episode and acknowledged how far they'd come – even more so when I told them I'd done it deliberately (their teacher in Year 3 had specifically told me not to put them together as they couldn't work collaboratively). Being this way was not meeting their needs, nor was it developing an appreciation of what it means to be an effective team worker.

Children want, need and deserve to be reliant on others and to have those same peers rely on them rather than their teachers. If they have self-respect they'll see how they can be of value. However, this is not a prompt to increase spoon-feeding for children across the land. Getting them to rely on others is not shorthand for not doing things for themselves, or opting out of work for a collaborative approach.

Moreover, the 4Bs Principle – Brain, Book, Buddy, Boss – supports this way of developing greater independence for the children. Through this they first learn to rely on themselves and their own work, seeking their own answers or understanding before turning to their classmates and, as a last resort, their teachers. This ensures that they learn in a connected and mutually supportive environment. This respect for relationships is how it should and must be – especially if you are to get homework completed, reviewed and developed without really setting it!

As a teacher, my job is to ensure that this happens consistently with a variety of people. You can check the success of this by the children's interactions, especially at lunch and breaktime. Because if it only happens in your room, when you're present, then it's not really embedded, is it? Furthermore, when it comes to seating plans, I change mine every half-term, thus establishing new learning partners and learning groups. The class have the right to discuss who is where, with whom they work and why, and understand that no pair may stay together for more than a term during the academic year.

This can be further supplemented by using the idea of 'jigsaw' group work, as championed by Robert Powell (Powell, 1997). I first heard about this at a conference in 1999. Jigsaw group work is where children have to work with others from a different group on their area of responsibility, before going back to their original group to feed back. This is ideal in both primary and secondary settings. I have used it to great effect in GCSE English classes to examine an extract from a text. During their time together, the children work on shared projects, peer-assess, edit each other's work and even take tests on behalf of each other: both take the test, but the randomly selected person's score counts for both. This all culminates in the final half-term when the children select their own partners. In my experience, a pair has never been chosen just for fun or been ignorant of the principles established since day one in September.

Establishing Relationships for Unhomework:

+ *Explain the seating choices you have made.* If you can't justify them, then why use them? This also teaches children to appreciate and understand the nature of their peers, respecting what they have to gain from each other.

+ *Two tests, one score.* The learning pairs prepare for a test together, but whoever's name is drawn out is the person whose score counts for both (they both take the test for comparative reasons). This also works for the children in learning some different ways of revising for tests from their peers. In primary schools this can be applied to mental maths and spelling tests, and in secondary schools it can be applied across all subjects.

- *Project-based learning (PBL).* Ensure this is used in conjunction with the PLTS team workers criteria, so that the children have a checklist and can self- and peer-assess their success and areas for development.

- *Marketplace.* This is a great way to share ideas and make creative use of 'plagiarism': getting children to share their 'I wish I'd thought of …' comments about their peers' work.

- *Online.* Use your school's VLE, Edmodo, Google Docs, Skype or alternative for peer collaboration outside of school where they can go online to share and solve problems.

Resilience

Kids nowadays, they don't make them like they used to.

Kano, 'Nobody Don't Dance No More'

Ann Masten, Professor of Child Psychology at Minnesota University, defines resilience as the positive capacity of people to cope with stress and catastrophe. It's being able to bounce back after an upset. Resilience, like self-esteem and self-confidence, is not something that children need to develop – it occurs naturally. However, its development can be hindered or negated by responses from significant others in their lives, and this can lead to a possible future deficit in some contexts.

According to Masten, being resilient has nothing to do with intelligence or gender; what matters is that children have 'the support of at least one parent perceived as caring, maintaining positive peer relationships from childhood to adolescence, and stability of adult love relationships' (Masten 2009: 224).

An important part of resilience is having some awareness of the future, of how things may turn out or what is likely to happen – this allows children to prepare for it in some way. However, much of what children do today is spent in immediacy, with no need for delayed gratification or persistent effort. But, if this way of thinking into the future is worked on throughout the year, in all subjects, the children will come to see that their efforts and the rewards are intimately linked to their own resilience; their habit of pushing forward when it would be easier to give up, and of thinking things through when they could seek quick and easy answers from others. When they have built up their peer relationships, they learn to see their resilience and emulate them. Without this strengthening of resilience, it is no wonder that when it comes to extended projects in older years many children cannot work to complete it from start to finish. They are continually asking for reassurance or giving up at the first challenge. Even worse, they are not fulfilling their potential, and are getting by just doing enough.

When we look at the ongoing disparity between male and female results, not only is it the perceived 'female friendly' curriculum but also the overused tick box approach that betrays boys in later years. The attitude of 'get it done and move on' – which is frequently instilled in boys – will suit the need for an evidence-based approach and then pervade their lives. Boys tend to be target driven, but look no further than that target. Rare is the boy who is keen to go further once they have met their target, be it a Grade C or Level 5. I have taught, mentored and discussed this with literally hundreds of boys and the common reply is, 'But that's my target, I've met it – why do I need to do more? I've passed, haven't I?' This is even when there is no pass or fail mark! Girls tend to scrutinise more and look beyond the target grade already achieved, checking that they have met every aspect of the grade. I recall a friend at sixth form, who on achieving two Grade As and a B, and so achieving her place at her desired university, bemused the head of sixth form by asking, 'Do you think I should defer a year and retake history [the B]?'

This target-driven culture starts with the Early Years Foundation Stage (EYFS) monitoring and continues throughout secondary school, reinforced by the media, which every summer focuses on the pass mark or percentage for a grade. The 2012 GCSE boundary changes illustrates this attitude. Children went into their exams, well prepared by their teachers, thinking they knew what they had to do to get a grade C or above; but after the exams were taken the grade boundaries were adjusted. After opening their results, imagine how many children said, 'I knew what I had to do and got that. Then "they" changed it.' In other words, they had done what they believed to be just enough to get their grade, and whilst for all concerned it must have been heartbreaking, this is evidence of focusing on a narrow target and doing just enough to get by.

By developing children as resilient learners, they will know their responsibilities and have the relationships to let them succeed. This requires putting more emphasis on securing the 5Rs through the work children do, starting in primary school, so that skills and knowledge go hand in hand. Each is a requirement of the other for developing a fully successful learner. Here is an example of this:

The Roman museum

Last year, with a changed curriculum, the subject was 'The Romans'. As we were starting from scratch with a new topic, I decided to make this into a project for my class, using an approach taken from Dorothy Heathcote's 'Mantle of the Expert', in which 'the class do all their curriculum work as if they are an imagined group of experts.'[2]

---

[2] See www.mantleoftheexpert.com for fuller details of the process, testimonials, training, etc.

I was introduced to this idea by a drama colleague when we were looking at how the curriculum could be reshaped back in 2008. The class were informed that they were responsible for transforming the room into a Roman museum and had a month to complete it. Immediately they recognised the class's strengths (Respect) and assigned roles and teams (Relationships) to tackle it, including inviting other classes to the grand opening and collaborating with their art teacher to work on their ideas.

Over four weeks they worked to achieve this. If work was not up to the standard they had decided upon the child was informed by the project's leaders (elected by them – Responsibilities) and given support to develop and change it. They would include nothing that they felt diminished the project as a whole. At the end of the year, the children cited this as one of their favourite parts of the year. Somewhat to the surprise of myself, my colleagues and their parents, the quality of work was much better than expected and the quantity was amazing too, proving Rushton Hurley correct:

If your students are sharing their work with the world they want it to be good. If they're just sharing it with you, they want it to be good enough.[3]

I firmly believe this approach is needed more widely; so much can be achieved by simply devising projects for the children. This has become one of the cornerstones of a different approach to homework. It ensures children have true responsibility for their education, so that they become the masters of their destinies.

---

3 As quoted on http://spotlight.macfound.org/blog/entry/playback-making-media-engaging-in-democracy-working-toward-the-future/

Establishing Resilience for Unhomework:

+ *Project-based learning.* Make work worthwhile and pertinent, but don't extend it so that it simply becomes the filler which gives you time to mark your GCSE coursework or complete reports.

+ *Apply the 'Mantle of the Expert'.* The children will gain a great sense of reward and it also prevents stifling the knowledge and skills they may already have to satisfy the scheme of work.

+ *In primaries use more secondary language.* By Key Stage 2 we should be referring to planning, drafting, editing and redrafting – not 'rough' and 'neat' work. Not only are these part of the English levels, but more importantly being neat isn't the be all and end all. Also, establishing the concept of rough work helps no one, especially boys.

+ *Time.* This really is simple: if you want children to stick at something then allow them the time to do so. Don't break into a healthy work session just because of a scheduled change. Work with colleagues to allow the children to continue to pursue what they are doing.

+ *Supported failure.* 'Failure' provides the opportunity for learning something new. If everything they do is easy or successful, are they challenging themselves? The phrase, 'Being stuck isn't a problem, staying stuck is,' is commonly heard in my room from September to October, then less and less as the children understand they can tackle the problem. Choose 'unGoogleable' work; something they have to aim for, knowing you're there for them (which relates back to respect and relationships).

Responsibilities

Children must recognise that they are responsible for their learning and that means they need to be given real and proper responsibility in school. This is especially the case in primary schools, where these qualities must be cemented in preparation for their teenage and adult lives. The roles too often assigned to young children, such as being line leader, line ender, register monitor and other prosaic titles, are merely box-ticking exercises for saying to the inspector, 'We give our children responsibility, and we instil citizenship values in them.' It's not that these roles are not important, it's just that they are not true responsibilities. For example, the register monitor who is reminded every day of the week that it's their turn to collect is not really being responsible at all. Similarly, the line leader who is there because they cannot behave and needs to be close to the teacher fools no one, especially not the children!

Responsibility supports the teaching of children's self-worth and values the role they have, which (as per PLTS) must change and develop with the project, assignment or group. In doing this they will learn to review their learning and be actively responsible for it, rather than being passive recipients of it. All that will do is restrict them to being children of our time, not their own. Remember the Hebrew proverb: 'Do not confine children to your own learning, for they were born in another time.'

It is our job to ensure that children can build and develop skills, traits and learning that will support them for their future in the twenty-first century, not for our past in the twentieth century.

There was a time in the 2008 academic year when, with no compulsory Key Stage 3 tests, work was going on across the country to look at how we could change the curriculum and truly prepare children for their later lives. This was led by the Specialist Schools and Academies Trust (SSAT) throughout that year and meant that children were included in the curriculum and delivery discussions, looking at the local wants and needs under a national and global framework, as well as those of the children themselves. The SSAT deployed regional teams with local support teachers (of which I was one) to demonstrate to other colleagues what could be done and to promote real examples from other schools where the curriculum was being radically changed due to Ed Balls's decision to scrap the tests. It was here that the idea of having a three-year Key Stage 4 really took shape across the country, allowing for breadth and depth of study – as well as the unforeseen consequence of multiple retakes for children to meet targets. Over time, as other pressures and an election took over, the project dissipated, though many of the links and changes continued.

In my experience of working with the SSAT, the children were almost always more innovative than the staff. In one conversation, staff and students were brainstorming ways of making the curriculum vibrant and exciting while still meeting the curriculum hours for each subject. One possible solution was to either cut humanities and languages hours, or extend the working day. The former solution was fairly popular with many children whilst the latter was universally unpopular. One of the children, Christina, asked, 'Well, why can't we be taught other subjects in French or German or Spanish?' Initially this was dismissed by many, but the Year 9 girl stuck to her guns and said, 'So children in those countries learn those lessons only in their own language do they? We could do numbers in maths, drama, food technology – actually, most things in a different language.' As others joined in the discussion and ideas were shaped and reformed, the curriculum did indeed change. In this, Christina could see how she had taken real responsibility for what was to happen in her studies and as one teacher said, 'She freed me of the shackles I'd put on myself.'

I still use this idea in my teaching. I love it when lessons are taught using Viking runes (once we have got to know them) or when we use Roman numerals in maths, which will at least give the children an appreciation of our Arabic number system now in use. The children enjoy it, see a relevance and, because it's memorable, it becomes embedded into their psyche. They will also use it when they teach each other (yes, my Year 4s deliver lessons to each other!). This not only includes lessons for review but also topics which we have not yet covered, and even things that are not in our curriculum but which interest them. They can do all of this in any way they like, which means we get Respect, Relationships, Resilience, Responsibilities and Rights all in one!

Establishing Responsibilities for Unhomework:

+ Instead of starting the year with your usual Ten Commandments speech, why not start the first term by asking them what rules they want for the year and what sanctions, if any, there should be? (I use a screenshot from John Sturges's 1960 film *The Magnificent Seven*. This allows me to play the music, outline the film's plot, and explain that all seven had a role, whatever their strength or weakness.)

+ For primaries: involve the class in deciding when they want to learn the non-specialist lessons. Would they rather have a couple of topic lessons throughout the week, or one extended period, or a blend of the two?

+ In secondaries: involve the children in decision-making concerning school governors, an active school council, charity week, working with younger years or involving younger years with their primary school. Extend this to work in the community – gardening, performances, shopping for the elderly, and so on.

Rights

At the mention of the word 'rights' I'm sure that some would immediately say that nowadays too many children know their rights rather than their responsibilities, and this is a good indicator of what's wrong with our society. This is shorthand for, 'Teach them their place and put them there, as we did until the 1960s!' However, whatever the media has to say on the matter, children do have rights which are coupled with their responsibilities, and these need to be taught. As the United Nations Universal Declaration of Human Rights states:

Article 26

1   Everyone has the right to education.

2   Education shall be directed to the full development of the human personality and to the strengthening of respect for human rights and fundamental freedoms. It shall promote understanding, tolerance and friendship among all nations, racial or religious groups, and shall further the activities of the United Nations for the maintenance of peace.

In fact, since 1992, after Britain's ratification and legal adoption of the United Nations Convention on the Rights of the Child, it has actually been a child's 'right to have their views respected, and to have their best interests considered at all times.' I wonder, does this really happen in all of our schools on a regular basis, let alone a daily or lesson-by-lesson basis? If the answer is no then we must do something and we must start with our own classrooms to make sure the children we work with do have this most basic of rights.

Admittedly, some colleagues will say (possibly as their class would say), 'But how can I make a difference by myself?' The African proverb says, 'If you think you're too small to make a difference, try sleeping in a room with a mosquito.'

There is the opportunity here to develop a greater understanding of the rights of others within their class and school, which makes conversations about respecting their peers, teachers and environment easier and more focused. Of paramount importance for any child must surely be their right to an education, so they should value and safeguard this with the utmost regard. When was the last time your children were taught about other countries where education is not seen as a right for everyone, regardless of what the UN has to say on the matter? Surely, the story of the shooting of Malala Yousafzai for protesting for an education in Pakistan provides at least a day's worth of material for any teacher, especially as Malala has been honoured with the International Children's Peace Prize. Such stories should serve to remind us how fortunate our children are being educated in Britain, not in the multitude of countries where the right to an education is not respected. Or in those where the technology we and our classes take for granted is a dream. Admittedly, Singapore, Finland or elsewhere may be the educationally successful flavour of the month, but with the correct focus, through understanding their rights, it will become clear to the children how lucky they are.

This understanding of rights should fundamentally underpin the class and school behaviour policy. Tolerance often appears to be the avenue here: 'It's X's SEN,' or, 'He's a boy,' or, 'Y can't help it,' or perhaps worst of all, 'Z has always been like that.' These are all justifications that I have heard. Why would any member of staff say such a thing, especially the last one? If they do, then probe a little to find out the real issue. However, should the children say it, then we're really in a sad place. To me, they should be remembering the other four Rs, and be willing to challenge any behaviour that impacts their right to an education – including that of the staff. A right to education comes with the responsibility of allowing others their right to one too.

An example of what I mean here is revealed by how I let my children work in the way in which they are most comfortable. This results in some children lying on the floor, some reversing chairs cowboy style and others kneeling, putting their books on their chairs. Some even like to stand. The ways are many and varied. Surprisingly, only two or three actually choose to sit 'properly' on their chairs. How is this sensibly achieved? There are two simple rules: 1) You can sit how you wish, but don't disturb the learning of others, and 2) You are working, so that means anyone lying on the floor can't be under the feet of others and those standing can't be in the way of others, and so on. It works! eight- and nine-year-olds respect each other enough to understand that they work best in different ways, and it doesn't become an issue with others doing it differently. (Of course, teaching colleagues do have an issue with this – 'That's not how they'll sit with me …' But funnily enough, the children can cope with the staff's individuality as well – which says much about the children, but probably more about the adults!)

Establishing Rights for Unhomework:

+ *Rules*. Allow the class to set or discuss the rules for themselves (as in Responsibilities). They then hold each other (and you) to account.

+ *Draw up a Class Charter (younger children will need support here).* Something like, 'We all have the right to … / We can all expect …'

+ *Expectations*. Include in the rights what they have a right to expect from you as the teacher.

+ *Show examples*. Such as where the right to education is not given, or other human rights abuses.

+ *Challenge*. Controversially, but worthwhile, deliberately ignore one of their rights and let them challenge you. Get them to argue their case about how you have been unfair and what is wrong. This works even better when you try to get other children onto your side and they side with someone else (Relationships!).

Assuming that the climate is right in your classroom and your children have the 5Rs (or suitable alternatives) ingrained in them, you can start not setting homework. This is not really about setting homework, but about getting great work from the children. In this you have to start small, whatever the age of your class, so that you can lead them to where you want them to be. Then you find yourself amazed as they take you somewhere else you'd never expected! For as Nelson Mandela says in his autobiography, *Long Walk to Freedom* (Mandela, 1994):

Education is the great engine of personal development. It is through education that the daughter of a peasant can become a doctor, that a son of a mineworker can become the head of the mine, that a child of farm workers can become the president of a great nation. It is what we make out of what we have, not what we are given, that separates one person from another.

Primary and secondary considerations

One question I am often asked about Unhomework is how it works with the different sectors. Given that I have taught from Year 4 to Year 13, I can honestly say that my approach is no different now in the primary sector than it was in the secondary. However, secondary-age children have shown themselves to need more support and encouragement as it is so different from the approach they are used to. The rest of this chapter outlines the process of introducing Unhomework to children in general, but is of greatest importance to secondary children. (Further support is given in Chapter 4 where I outline how to convince others about your new approach. The arguments I adduce there are applicable to the children, who will frequently ask similar questions about exams, pertinence and future relevance.)

For primary colleagues, whilst I am saddened that homework is set at all to the children in this sector, many of the ideas I outline can be used at any age; however, I believe this works best starting at Year 4. I would encourage Year 3 teachers to begin the process as the academic year progresses, especially in the Summer Term, in preparation for Year 4. This will allow Year 4 to springboard immediately with learning and Unhomework which will not be alien to them, particularly as they will already have new teachers and classmates to become accustomed to. Many children in primary schools will complete Unhomework inadvertently with things such as Show and Tell, or by researching something they are interested in. My advice is to encourage this both in the individual and in the whole class. Do not shut down those 'Miss, did you know ...' statements because they are not relevant to what is being done at that time. Instead, embrace them and celebrate them – they are the very essence of Unhomework.

Introducing Unhomework (the DAD Model)

It would be easy but overly simplistic to separate the messages for both educational phases and to try to treat them in isolation, but I think that for each sector the approach needs to employ the same three-step DAD process:

D = Discuss – with the class, tell them how things will be.

A = Apply – get them doing homework for themselves, working with their parents.

D = Discuss – with the children and parents, in a follow-up and as they ask questions.

This was best exemplified when I started at my current school. Moving from the state secondary sector to an independent primary school was baffling for some people to comprehend, though being a parent at the school did ease things. When you want to try new things, there can be an air of suspicion about your reasons, especially if 'we don't do it like that' is a pervasive attitude. However, having frequently complained about how I would like Year 7s to enter secondary school knowing Unhomework, this was my chance to try it out and I wasn't going to miss it!

Checking the school's homework policy, I knew that work had to be set nightly (except for Friday – we don't set homework for the weekend), but it didn't say by whom. Clearly, it was expected the teacher would set it – so that was my first step. The second was to raise the level of challenge with the class, slipping into conversations and lessons how something they were doing was similar, or even the same as something I had done with GCSE classes. This then allowed me to follow the DAD process. Over the early weeks I set work on the title only, or a task with multiple possible outcomes, but I wanted the children to fully experience Unhomework for themselves.

I remember it clearly – I decided that the first, full Unhomework to do with the children was going to be maths, so at the start of the lesson I had the following on the board:

'What do you need to improve? What are you doing about it?'

The children discussed the first question with their learning partners and then we had a range of topics, from tables to charts, through to area and volume. 'Right,' I said. 'Now think about what you will do to tackle it. That's what I want you to do.' The classroom buzzed with conversations and a flurry of hands went up:

'Can I do what I want?'

'Do I have to write it down?'

'Am I allowed to work with someone else?'

'Can I video myself?'

These are just some of the questions I was asked. I answered each one and we had a thorough discussion about all of them. I explained that the children needed to decide what they were going to work on, when it would be given in and what their success criteria was. They worked independently; my TA and I circulated the room but they first turned to their learning partners and sets to check things out. Some of the examples they came up with were making a model to understand area and volume, baking a cake for measuring and time, creating a coloured multiplication table and writing a story for fractions. The children understood what they were doing and all of them had given at least three nights for completion. Explaining that this was a very grown-up way of working, I told them that they would need to tell their mums and dads what was going on, but I would be in class by 8 a.m. the next morning to answer any questions.

Sure enough, at 8 a.m. several parents were there; some to ask questions, others to bring in their child's work, as they had all been so inspired they had gone straight home and done it that night. Harry, who had written a song for tables, brought in an iPod with the recording and as he set it up his dad told me, 'He's never been so keen to do homework – normally he takes no time at all on it.' The tales from other parents were similar, with one exception. One girl had wanted to improve her measuring and converting by using jugs of water at home, adding and subtracting them. Her dad came in convinced she'd lied to him and said, 'It's okay, Mr Creasy, I went on the Internet and downloaded a sheet, she's done that.' I'm not sure who was more horrified: the children there who told him Ashley hadn't lied, or the dad at what he'd done!

After assembly we discussed the homework. I reiterated the message about it being okay to complete the work early, as long as the quality was good, and we galleried the work. The children asked some questions, a common one being, 'But what if we decide to do something else, not what we said we'd do?' I explained it was their work and as long as they did what they needed to, I didn't mind. And from there, Unhomework started fully in my Year 4 room for the academic year of 2010!

By doing this you get to the heart of the matter immediately, as you are tackling the children's understanding of this different approach. Do not underestimate your class's need for the opportunity to air concerns and to ask questions. Many of them will have been indoctrinated with ideas of how homework should be done, especially at secondary school; not only by previous teachers, but also by their parents. If you do not tackle this and help them appreciate this new style then they will not understand it before they apply it, and worse, they will not be able to explain it to their parents and convince them these changes are for the best.

Wanna be startin' somethin'? – setting homework in the early weeks:

- Give plenty of time for completion (handing in early is only good if the work has been given the due accord – otherwise hand it back to them, unmarked).

- Expect high standards (and so learn what they are capable of!).

- Check their progress towards completion – they need to ask for clarification (DAD Model).

- Make your first homework 'This is me'. Allow any format for completion. The children present themselves to you in their own way. This will show you their interests and how they like to present their work. In secondary, if other colleagues are doing this too, tell them it's fine to use the same work twice. You both need a copy; there is no point duplicating work unnecessarily. Some might think that if different teachers want the same work it should be repeated but in different formats. That, in my opinion, is a waste of time and effort.

- Ensure a variety of task styles. Have work where things can be drawn; models can be made; stories, poems or songs can be written; a dance can be performed; or where PowerPoint or Prezi can be used. For a title such as 'The Water Cycle', all of the above are applicable.

- Have levelled homework – Bronze, Silver, Gold and Platinum work to create appropriate challenges for the children – and see who takes what. You may be surprised! Wait to see who asks for the level beyond Platinum (and, unfortunately perhaps, the one who asks for below Bronze!).

- Have a homework amnesty – don't set any homework one night, except for the children having to talk about what they did with their gained time in the next lesson.

- Get the children to set the marking criteria for homework, and then get them to mark each others' work to those criteria.

- In your plenary, ask the children what could be done to further the learning in a lesson. Vote on the best idea – that's the homework. Even though this negates the mantra that all homework must be set at the start of a lesson, it allows the empowerment of the children, which is the whole idea!

The first few weeks of Unhomework

At this stage it is important to remind yourself that you are doing this because you know it is better than setting homework in the traditional manner. It is likely that several children will find it hard going at first to do things differently. However, by taking your time to secure the right climate for learning through the 5Rs and by introducing homework in a different manner, as outlined above, the children (certainly by

October) should be ready to experience Unhomework. And with your careful and considered support and encouragement they will be able to do so with confidence.

Early steps in Unhomework:

1   Run a homework lottery. If a child is selected, they have the choice whether to complete the homework or not (this certainly alerts them to the fact things are different!).

2   Run an 'unlottery'. If a child is selected, they have to complete the homework. This works even better if you run the lottery and then toss a coin as to whether it's a lottery to do or not to do homework!

3   Give title-only homework. This is a task with a multitude of ways of completing it. The 'This Is Me' exercise is an ideal example, as is the task title, 'Safety', in science, which the children can meet in any way they choose.

4   Offer a homework menu (see 'Mission: Homework' in Appendix 2). The children work for several weeks using a range of options, all of which are allocated points. The children aim to meet the target total which has been identified for them, accumulated from the range of tasks they choose to complete.

5   Offer a range of homework with children selecting their preferred one.

6   What's your target? The children set their own work based on their targets. In my experience, they seem to have quite a number of these.

7   What can't you do? As the name suggests, the children use homework time to tackle something they can't do. I find that this works particularly well if you are able to tackle something new too. It was from this that I learned to juggle!

8   Peer set. Once they have been schooled in the art of Unhomework, the children set it for each other. This will allow you to pinch their ideas for future use. You could even let yourself go and allow the children to set you some homework too. This encourages them to be creative (provided you have the right climate in your class) and shows that you practise what you preach. For example, one year I had to deliver class expectations to the tune of 'Call Me Maybe'!

By changing how you work with their children, parents will soon come to appreciate the opportunities you are providing for them – for being actively involved in their child's learning and for understanding what it is they're doing and how. The earlier this occurs in a child's education the better; in this way good habits are developed by everyone. It would be ideal if this were part of the secondary transfer process or part of the induction for children into secondary schools, so that there is a seamless flow between the sectors. Thus, if colleagues in primary school have cemented these ideas, they can be built on in secondary school, rather than simply ignored because 'That's not how we do it,' or started all over again, because the primary children have always received simple, unchallenging work and have not undertaken independent, extended tasks.

These very simple steps, based on the lessons elsewhere in the book, are the first I use in beginning to not set homework for the children, and provide the basis for the successful development of Unhomework. This opens up their minds to how things can be done differently. Invariably, even the lottery winners do the homework! And that is key, because all of a sudden the children have an ownership over their homework which they never had before, given that they had always been instructed to complete *x* homework, by *y* date and given *z* target to achieve.

Essentially then, the whole thing is about a mindset (yours and your classes') and can be exemplified like this:

Yes, I did it!

I will do it

I can do it

I'll try to do it

How do I do it?

I want to do it

I can't do it

I won't do it

Which step have you reached today?

Within all of our classes, children can be at any step of the diagram at any time, some transitioning between them throughout the learning experience you are providing for them. The challenge for us is to ensure that we achieve the top four stages, having reassured them that they can, answering the questions about 'how to do it?' (Look again at the DAD Model.)

Establishing Unhomework

Once the children have developed their understanding and are confident with the concept of Unhomework they will be ready to take it further. Obviously, with a class of individuals this will occur at different times, so in the spirit of Unhomework it is important that the children are treated individually by supporting them to the next stage only when they are ready for it. This can push others to take it further too, as they see their peers reach a par with them and so want to re-establish the gap by striving to achieve more! As long as this is not conducted in a derogatory or belittling manner, it is a powerful tool. Some ways I have used to build on the foundations are:

- *Well I never.* The children think of one thing they've always wanted to try and tackle it. This is best supported by you doing the same, as I did with the juggling. YouTube learning can be a wonderful tool to help you!

- *Project work.* This much underused tool offers real and purposeful project work. When project work is done properly, the children take on clearly defined roles and set their own work to ensure they meet the goal or deadline. I like to use this as a cross-curricular piece – I work in the primary sector, after all. For secondary schools it takes a little more organising; subject, department or team collaboration will be of great use to you, your colleagues and the children. The Roman museum project I referred to earlier is a great example, but if you're stuck search the Internet for ideas for group work, or put out a request on Twitter and there'll be plenty of people happy to help (best used in conjunction with the PLTS sheet in Appendix 1).

- *Project work again.* Repeat the above, ensuring that the children undertake different roles, especially as some may be able to utilise class time to be able not to do homework. Relax – this is fine too. Just think how many colleagues manage their time well, whilst others seem to take a never-ending supply of marking and preparation home. This is a great life skill and also allows you to see what they prefer!

- *You're the teacher.* The children prepare to teach a lesson; their great challenge is for them to deliver this to younger children. Sure, some will wing it, but their peers soon winkle them out and can be merciless in their assessments – especially the ones who really worked hard! This also makes for a good discussion; just think who their role model may have been before you start it – it can be embarrassing having your worst habits played out in front of you as you watch!

Unhomework Utopia

Depending on the age of the class, you may have several years of traditional homework to battle against. I find working with Year 5/6 children is easier as they are less indoctrinated – though one does have to tackle greater parent attitudes. However, it works across the age range and I have initiated this with children up to and including GCSE level.

When it works perfectly, the process is as follows:

The child:

1   Decides on what needs doing.

2   Sets an appropriate homework to tackle this.

3   Creates the criteria for assessment.

4   Completes the work by their own deadline.

5   Performs a self-review of the work.

6   The child's learning partner peer-assesses the work and a discussion about progress takes place.

7   Work and assessments are shared (often via a 'marketplace') and others provide input.

8   Teacher support is given if needed and the process repeats.

The great thing about this is that once the class have been assisted into it, they can then run the whole thing by themselves and undertake the independent learning which will equip them for lifelong learning. This also allows children to develop their own work which has nothing to do with the curriculum. I recently witnessed children from my previous year's class sharing the work they were doing (which had nothing to do with their current learning) simply because they wanted a challenge beyond what they were doing in class with their current teacher.

CHAPTER THREE
PARENTS AND UNHOMEWORK

Parents' role in homework

Scenario 1

Parent: What homework have you got tonight?

Child: It's okay, I've done it at school.

Parent: Can I see it? I need to sign your planner to say you've done it.

Child: I've already given it in; it was only finishing stuff off.

Parent: Isn't there anything else to do?

Child doesn't respond; they've already walked off and parent goes back to what they were doing, resigned to this status quo.

Scenario 2

Parent: How much homework have you got?

Child: Just a bit of stuff from this sheet.

Parent: Is that it?

Child: That's more than enough. I want some time to myself to chill.

Parent: I've a good mind to complain. You need more homework than that. You chill quite enough in my opinion!

Child: What? You can't be serious! You're so embarrassing. Don't you dare. Everyone will just laugh at me when they find out.

Parent: I don't care about them; I'm only worried about you and your future. You're my main concern. I know in my day we …

Scenario 3

Parent: How much homework have you got?

Child: Oh don't, I'll be here hours.

Parent: That's ridiculous, when will you have time to be a child? What about your clubs and time with your friends?

Child: Tell me about it. Everyone's saying this year is way harder than any other.

Parent: I've a good mind to complain; you can't do all of that, you'll suffer burnout and stress!

Child: What? You can't be serious! You're so embarrassing. Don't you dare; everyone will just laugh at me. I'll just have to cope, somehow.

Parent: I don't care about them, I'm only worried about you and your future, you're my main concern. I know in my day we …

These scenarios are just three variations that are played out in homes across the country on a nightly basis. I can best describe parents' attitudes to homework as a Goldilocks issue. For some it's too much, for others never enough, and for the less concerned remainder it's just about right. This view is supported not only by a recent survey at my school, but also by the numerous conversations I have had with parents throughout my teaching career and the information I have received from colleagues across the country teaching in both sectors.

In his research between 1987 and 2003, Professor Harris Cooper cited the 10-Minute Rule,[1] whereby children should receive ten minutes per night commensurate with their year group or grade of education. Whilst I would question what suitable, stimulating and challenging work can be achieved in this overly prescriptive time frame, the very nature of the broad brush approach applied here ignores the academic, social and age differences which are applicable within a class, let alone a year group. This would suggest that a different approach is required.

It is through Unhomework that I have witnessed and been told by parents that they have had the opportunity to play a more pivotal role in working with their child in a more natural manner and in a way they prefer. I have found this to be especially true in earlier years, where parents can build a strong learning relationship with their child. This relationship will develop as the child grows older. Even when I have introduced Unhomework for Year 10 and 11 children it has had a huge positive impact at home. This happens because Unhomework is not seen as subtracting from the precious time parents spend with their children of an evening or weekend, but as a fundamental part of it.

As a parent, I appreciate the demands on a parent's time only too well. What matters is setting your priorities for what you want for your child. Yes, exam results are important. Yes, life success is important too. But – and this

---

1 http://en.wikipedia.org/wiki/Homework

is a fairly big but – when parents are surveyed about their children, the top two factors (way ahead of success) are firstly their child's happiness, and secondly their child's safety. Therefore, it is the duty of every parent that they themselves – not a childminder, au pair or nanny, and certainly not the child's friends – are the prime focus for maintaining their education for as long as possible. If children are going to develop the 5Rs and learn a different way of doing homework from the one their parents undoubtedly experienced at school, then the children will need parental help. In the rest of this chapter I will show how the school can support you in doing this, as well as ways in which you can model Unhomework with your child and make it a natural part of your everyday lives.

How to introduce Unhomework to parents (the MUM Model)

The key element here is effective communication, because without this Unhomework may fail, or certainly not fulfil the beliefs and philosophy behind it. The parents should notice a difference and start to feel differently about their child's learning.

It is in this area of communication where the disparity between primary and secondary sectors comes into sharp focus. For primary school colleagues, communication should be fairly easy, as the drop-off and pick-up points in the day allow opportunities for you and parents to meet and chat about concerns. By their very nature primary schools tend to be more inviting and welcoming to parents, who feel more able to access their child's education and classroom (often to search for lost items!) and to engage in informal conversations. It is at these times that you will have the perfect opportunity to answer questions about what is happening. This will give you a relaxed way of supporting the parents through the homework–Unhomework transition and to explain how and why it's necessary.

For secondary colleagues this informal communication can be trickier, especially as there is no daily gathering of parents in the playground. This means that being as accessible as possible is of paramount importance. It is better to have meetings with the parents early in the school year, rather than waiting until a parents' evening at the end of term. Furthermore, secondary colleagues are more likely to work within a subject department structure which can make things trickier for them to communicate at the end of the school day.

Given these apparent differences, each scenario needs careful handling to recognise their individuality. Although the primary playground allows direct access to parents for getting your message across, it can also be a hive for gossip spreading, and the message gets diluted and altered if not delivered in a considered and consistent manner.

Both educational phases need to use the same three-step MUM process (to complement the DAD Model in Chapter 2):

M = Must – it is vital that both parents and children know this.

U = Understand – without the necessary understanding, Unhomework will falter.

M = Methods – by using a variety of ways of completing homework the diverse and individual approach of Unhomework becomes apparent.

The DAD Model – Discuss–Apply–Discuss – allows you to get to the heart of the matter immediately by assessing the children's understanding of this different approach. Do not underestimate the need for your class to air concerns and ask questions, as many will have been indoctrinated by previous teachers and their parents about how homework should be done. If you do not address this and help them to appreciate this new way of doing things they will not understand it before they are expected to apply it. Far worse, they will not be able to explain Unhomework to their parents or convince them these changes are for the best.

The MUM process is also important in that it allows the different approach to be exemplified to parents, experienced by the learner and supported through experience. Your class's parents can only support their children when they have the correct understanding. You need to share with them your philosophy of independent and self-derived work that will improve and build on both the child's strengths and areas for development. The parents will then be able to encourage and support them themselves. They will quickly come to see that Unhomework is neither a fad, nor a way of generating an easy life for the teacher or the child, but that it provides valuable learning activities which they can take part in, enjoy and which will deliver a lifelong benefit to the child.

How can parents further support their children?

When I worked in the secondary phase, there came a time – often around Year 8 or 9, although sometimes earlier – when many parents bemoaned, 'I just can't seem to talk to them any more.' But maybe they don't realise that they never really did in the first place. Children soon learn to escape into their make-believe worlds rather than engage in conversation with their parents. Even when members of the family are all in the same place at the same time, there are often distractions such as TV, mobile phones, computers and so on, which keep individuals locked into their own world. For some parents, who are not in the habit of turning off these distractions, learning to engage in proper conversation with their children could be a challenge. It means not only talking about their own experiences, but asking questions, being curious and enjoying banter. Parents need to ensure a greater balance in their child's life. They can do this by enriching their language, challenging and provoking their thinking and understanding, and by making sure they have as many diverse experiences as possible. Parents need to actively support them in engaging in activities (especially clubs) outside of what is seen as their comfort zone.

Above all, parents need to show their children that they are loved and special. I'm not talking about the type of 'love' exhibited by an angry parent storming on stage to challenge Simon Cowell's lack of belief in their child's caterwauling when they think they ought to be a singing star. No, I mean the type of love and belief in them that's rooted in genuine care, affection and support; love for who they are, can be and want to be. It's love that provides the child with the recognition of the power they have over the choices they make in their lives, choices which will have future impacts, sometimes decisively so.

If done correctly, this means that the Unhomework way of working can easily be incorporated into parents' time with their child, which, according to a 2004 Harvard Graduate School of Education study, is what parents want.[2] This ideal will, in turn, lead the children to realise that homework is not just what is set for them, but their responsibility as they then begin to independently lead their own learning. This is wholeheartedly supported by a study titled 'Homework in the Home' by Garth Sundem (reported in *Psychology Today* in 2012[3]) which showed that children achieve best when parents support their autonomy, as opposed to leading, or worse completing, the work for their child. After all, if homework really is to support and encourage lifelong learning, children require the autonomy to make errors. With support they can learn and complete homework so that gradually the props of parents (and teachers) can be gently eased away as and when necessary – but reinstalled should the challenge require them.

2 http://www.gse.harvard.edu/hfrp/projects/fine/resources/research/homework.html

3 http://www.psychologytoday.com/blog/brain-trust/201202/homework-help-hurts-learning

Five simple ways a parent can support their child's learning:

1   Talk with your child.

2   Listen with genuine interest.

3   Ask them questions (but not just questions you already know the answer to; show your ignorance and willingness to learn).

4   Know what they're interested in. Remember that it might be different from what you expect (or even want).

5   Work together to develop their love of learning. Stimulate and engage them, support them in new things.

Furthermore, it is important to do these things from an early age and incorporate this as an expected part of the daily and weekly routine. In this way there is less likelihood of disengagement when the child gets older. Too often parents speak of their teenage child as having a double-O prefix and maintaining a stiff-upper-lip silence that James Bond would envy, not divulging any secrets from their school day beyond, 'It's all right,' or, 'Nothing much,' or simply a grunt, when in actual fact the parents provided their basic training since their formative age! It is not for nothing that Jesuits believe 'Give me the child until he is seven and I will give you the man.'

This all sounds good, doesn't it? But how exactly should it be done? In the table below is a list of Do's and Don'ts for successfully supporting your child's learning:

Do	Don't
Know what they are learning about	Talk about the differences to 'your day'
Listen to them read every day[4]	Multitask as you listen
Ask them questions (the 6Ws and 8WT[5])	Show off your knowledge
Give them varied experiences	Make it all about expense
Show them they can achieve	Ignore things they can't do[6]

4 This is forgotten by many parents as soon as the child completes their school's reading scheme, but a daily reading session is a great opportunity to spend time with them. Coupled with this is the need for you to read to them regularly, so they can learn from hearing and simply enjoy the experience. In September 2013, numerous articles and advice from the National Association of Headteachers (NAHT) appeared which showed that a third of parents never read to their child, nor do they do anything to combat the many distractions in their child's life in order to take part in this simple activity with them (see www.theguardian.com/society/2013/sep/13/parents-distracted-children-mobiles-headteachers).

5 6Ws focuses on the questions: What? Where? When? Why? Who? How? The How is vital as it allows for exploration of feelings and emotions and is a good way (along with others) of planning stories/essays. 8WT = 8Way Thinking. This is a way of questioning and investigating subjects and topics with different emphasis, using eight concepts (I tend to pair them up myself), based on Gardner's multiple intelligences: words and numbers, sights and sounds, people and places, and actions and feelings. (See http://www.independentthinking.co.uk/Cool+Stuff/8Way+Thinking/default.aspx for a more detailed exposition). These two simple methods provide low-stress, easy-going learning opportunities.

6 Picasso said, 'I am always doing that which I cannot do, in order that I may learn how to do it.' This is a challenge for most people. Teach your children by example, so they see you trying things you haven't done before. If you just do what's easy for you, you can inadvertently deter them as they think, 'I can't do that,' or, 'I can't do it that well,' and then dismiss the whole thing with, 'Why bother?'

Further activities to support learning

The following ideas are all practical ways to work with your children. None requires teachers to set homework; they are things that any parent can do with their child and will allow greater development for the child. Nor do they require extra time than that which you have already. However, they do need your input. It is not a good idea to allow children to work by themselves on these activities as you carry on with other tasks. If you do these kinds of activities as a normal part of family life you will be enhancing your relationship with your child as they grow up. These activities also address the different types of intelligence your child has. The hardest part for you may be in letting them take the lead and make mistakes, but that's the way they will be learning the most. I still struggle when my daughter doesn't start a jigsaw by completing the outside pieces before the inside! At least that shows me some of the patterns of behaviour that drive my way of doing things and it makes me realise how other people do things differently.

Although you will be letting them take the lead, the list below is a set of ideas to get you started. Some will work better than others at different times. The best plan is to start early and then build upon them, once they have become part of the parent routine. There is little to be gained just by doing them once in a blue moon; nor is there much value in spending every minute you have with your children in some kind of structured activity! We all need quiet time, time to ponder, time to 'do nothing'. Also remember to revisit things to see how they change. Just because something doesn't work one day, that doesn't mean it won't work in the future.

15 ways to help your children develop learning skills

1   *Reading.* Do this every day, using different types of text. Walter Dean Myers puts this best, 'If you had a sick patient, you wouldn't try to entice them to medicine, you'd tell them flat out "take this or you're going to die". We need to tell kids flat out: reading is not optional.'[7] (See the Do's and Don'ts list above.)

2   *Cooking.* The process of cooking covers English, maths, science, art, history (if you let it) and geography, as well as providing them with practical life skills.

3   *DIY.* This provides numerous opportunities for problem solving, measurement, spatial ability, maths, following instructions.

4   *Gardening.* This supports naturalistic learners, teaches care and patience and long-term planning.

5   *Board games.* Playing games teaches taking turns and playing to rules. It shows that having rules makes play more enjoyable and creative. It also supports accepting that you don't always win.

6   *Computer games.* If you are not familiar with these your children can show you how to play! If you are already a gamer then don't show off your superior skills. Always give them a chance to beat you, and take time afterwards to think of how you could have done better. Sharing a computer game helps develop resilience and perseverance, as well as improving your reaction times. It will also allow you to show you aren't the best at everything. Whilst I dread Just Dance on the Wii, my daughter loves it. I have to admit that it's great exercise – and a mild form of humiliation for me leaves her feeling great!

7 http://www.publishersweekly.com/pw/by-topic/childrens/childrens-industry-news/article/50033-walter-dean-myers-named-national-ambassador-for-young-people-s-literature.html

7   *Jigsaws.* A good way to develop spatial acuity, persistence and problem solving. It also allows time to chat at ease as you collaborate together.

8   *Pets.* The great thing about looking after pets is that it teaches the child to develop their caring and nurturing instincts; it also gives them something worthwhile to share information about with friends.

9   *Television.* What does your child watch? Do you watch with them? What was the last news or documentary programme you viewed together? Do you turn off the TV and talk about what you have just seen? There are many programmes that can teach much about life and getting along with others.

10 *Internet.* There is something to be said for the serendipity that arises when you follow a trail on the Internet, but sometimes what you discover is not reliable! How can you teach your child to discriminate the good from the nonsense? You can stick to more reliable sites, such as bbc.co.uk, nationalgeographic.com (with its kids' version: nationalgeographic-kids.co.uk), nasa.com, New Scientist for Kids (www.sciencenewsforkids.org) or museum websites. Sites like www.kidsites.com also offer links to choices on many different types of site.

11 *Culture.* Make museum and art gallery visits, not only to engage with what your child is learning but also to stimulate their enjoyment and your own.

12 *Singing.* Sing songs together on a car journey (this may only last until a certain age). It is fun and provides an excellent opportunity to examine the lyrics. For example, as an Elvis fan, 'Heartbreak Hotel' is perfect for discussing extended metaphors with older children.

13 *Road signs and billboards.* These are great for initiating discussions about advertising and geography.

14 *Number-plate countdown.* Make words which include the letters on the car in front. Pick three cars and use the numbers to create a sum of their choice. Better still, they think of it and you have to solve it.

15 *Word games.* We're spoilt for choice here but a good example for starters is Alphabet. Give ten words starting with a given letter. This can also be varied to go through the alphabet giving animals or countries or foods, and so on. Or you could try word association (Mallet's Mallet to those of us of a certain age).

These are all easy and, on the whole, free ways for engaging your child. They will also help prepare them for future learning.

CHAPTER FOUR
CONVINCING COLLEAGUES

'You're doing what?'

This was a common question posed by colleagues when I established Unhomework with my classes. They were incredulous that the status quo of homework was to be challenged, indeed dismantled. It took a while for this attitude to change. My colleagues began observing me and discussing Unhomework. Once they had seen how it works they became convinced that I was on to a good thing, and many went on to change the way they delivered homework themselves. This chapter aims to support you in being able to counter the points that colleagues will undoubtedly have about the veracity of your new approach, and how, with the right approach, you can convert them too.

The key to all of this is to be secure both in your understanding of your philosophy and in the belief that Unhomework is the way forward; to be certain that it offers accelerating progress towards true independence and secures the lifelong learning skills that we teachers desire to embed within our classes over their time with us.

I have found that if you are certain and congruent about your *raison d'être* for Unhomework, if you can clearly expound its virtues as part of your overall learning package for the children, then staff will be convinced. However, if it comes across as a bit of a cop-out for the children doing work or as a way of avoiding doing marking

– which I have seen cause greater chagrin with colleagues – then, understandably, people will never be convinced. Simply put, Unhomework should be seen as a simple yet obvious extension to your core educational beliefs about how children learn best and how you deliver that in your classroom. Imagine yourself as a stick of Blackpool rock: if you were cut in half, what would people see running throughout your core? Does Unhomework blend with your flavour or does it clash? You see, convincing people about the benefits of Unhomework depends on:

1   Everything you say.

2   Everything you do.

3   Ensuring (1) and (2) are consistent and complementary, whatever the pressures or demands.

Potential challenges

Yeah, but, no, but ... I just can't believe you just said that.

Vicky Pollard, *Little Britain*

This catchphrase may well represent the words you will hear from colleagues when your use of Unhomework begins to spread around the school. In my own experience, this is more likely to happen when the homework traditionalists teach your Unhomeworkers the following lesson, or year, depending on your teaching phase. Not being used to Unhomework, your colleagues will hear the children's delight at being given real responsibility and freedom in setting their work, criteria and deadline and not be able to believe it.

It is best to deliver Unhomework as if you expect to be seen as the one who has had it all so wrong in the past. Duh! Why didn't I think of getting children to think for themselves before!

There will be some members of staff who will judge Unhomework unfavourably and make up their minds without ever discussing it with you or seeking to understand why you are doing this. That is fine too. It's their choice and you have to accept it – after all, that is part of the philosophy you are expounding. And that means that as you introduce your reasoning, clearly acknowledge that there are different ways of approaching this challenge. If you simply ignore them in a self-satisfied manner, knowing you're right, then you have missed the point entirely! You have to walk your talk. Placating others by watering down the ideas is the coward's way out. It doesn't move the discussion forward, nor does it spread Unhomework further. If you believe what you're doing is best for the children then surely you want it to become part of other colleagues' lessons? In addition, simply ignoring those staff who are not on your wavelength also prevents your thinking from being challenged, which can lead to isolationism and

enmity, and still Unhomework does not go beyond your own classroom.

The alternative? Well, this is where you find the greatest challenge. Somehow you would need to clearly engage colleagues in dialogue about your means and methods and explain your thinking before you start the process yourself. At this stage you don't have any results to demonstrate, only your enthusiasm, which can easily be a stumbling block.

Over the years I have rehearsed this scenario many times and I'm hoping that my experience will help you prevent a negative outcome or response happening to you. Remember that this is not a one-off, nor a mere whim. You'll have many occasions for learning from the responses you get. Presenting Unhomework is not always easy to do and ironically, as I have found, a staffroom is often the last place that teaching and learning and the sharing of ideas occurs! It's a break for the staff, often their way of retreating into their own world. I have worked in schools where I am convinced that whole terms have passed and learning has not been discussed once in the staffroom, other than a teacher complaining about the child or class who has ruined a perfectly planned lesson.

Notwithstanding this, take advantage of the opportunities that arise; praise the work your children have produced using Unhomework. Ensure that other teachers can see the results you are getting. Talk to subject leaders and teachers of other subjects to see what they are doing and discuss ways you can utilise that too. By adopting a subtle approach, rather than being brash and boastful, you are more likely to show staff that Unhomework is a considered and well-thought-out process – one that leads to enhanced learning practices and will have an impact on all of the children, not just in the time you have with them but beyond.

That is not to say that every teacher will be convinced. I have found that when you discuss Unhomework with them staff will fall into one of three camps:

1   *Enthusiasts*. These people like the idea, want to engage with it further, and, wherever possible, observe the teaching that you do so that they can trial it for themselves. This allows informal learning pairs or triads to evolve.

2   *Cautious enthusiasts*. These people like the idea but either feel it's not for them or it's too risky. However, they are open-minded and prepared to see evidence of how it can work. They may often feel that they lack the experience or expertise to carry it off, even when they've observed it, because you make it look so easy. The best way to develop these colleagues is to not only discuss it with them but to get them working alongside an enthusiast, someone who has already converted to Unhomework. That way they can discuss pitfalls and share emotions along the way and have you supporting them.

3   *Pessimists.* These are the easiest to identify. You probably know who they'd be in your staffroom now. Per-haps your instinct would be to ignore them and to work with the others who want to develop Unhome-work, but that's not in the spirit of the process. You may also find that should a pessimist (or two) converse with a cautious enthusiast, the tide will have turned for them! The best advice is to find out what their deep issue is. The longer you've been at a school, the more likely it is that you will know something of the pessimist's history. You should still chat to them, remain friendly and amiable, and keep chipping away.

Below are some of the comments I have received and how I have answered them, which I think you'll find help-ful. However, the best help will come from the children, which I detail at the end of the chapter, but is aptly demonstrated here.

This was overheard in a classroom which happened to be adjacent to where I was working – I wasn't sure whether to smile or cry!

'Miss, do we have to do a poster about the water cycle?'

'What does it say on the board?'

'Well, I can see that it says create a poster, but …'

'Then if it says that, what do you think you have to do?'

'No, I know that, but …'

'Why are you arguing? That's your first warning. Copy down the homework.'

'It's just that …'

'You clearly want a second warning. Well, well done, you have it.'

'But I have written it down, all I am asking is if I can't do something else – do I have to do a water cycle poster?'

'What do you mean something else? That's the homework – what do you have in mind?'

'Well, I could write a poem or an account from a raindrop's point of view, I could make a model, or a video of the cycle. I could paint a picture or create a Prezi.'

'What nonsense, just complete the homework I've set and stop talking. We need to move on.'

'Mr Creasy used to let us create our own work, Miss, I just thought …'

'Ah, that letting you set your own work thing. Nonsense! And no, you didn't think. If you'd thought, you'd have stopped arguing. That's your third warning – go outside.'

'Okay, but can I ask one last question, then I'll go and stop asking.'

'What?!'

'As long as I do your poster, do you mind if I do something more exciting and interesting too?'

'Fine, just do the poster, now out!'

Door shuts.

'Miss, can I do something else too?' five children chorus!

At break the colleague came in and asked me directly, 'I guess you heard all that?' I couldn't deny it, but this then led to a discussion about the how and why of Unhomework and led to her admitting she didn't want to lose control; she'd been put on capability a while before and didn't want to return to that. She felt Unhomework would cede her authority to the children and standards would slip, and then she saw a pit of inevitability. The best thing was when she said, 'Mark, I'd like to do it, but ...' I stopped her and told her she'd taken the first step and said we'd work on it together. Sometime later that term, when she'd built her confidence up, she delivered her first Unhomework. She simply said,

---

'In your planners write how you're going to take the learning further. You choose how you'll show this and how it will be marked. I think a reasonable time limit is no more than three weeks, if that's okay?'

Next door, unbeknown to the children, I was smiling; I knew how much it had taken for her to do that. All was well in the world until I heard,

---

'Someone's been taking lessons from Creasy!'

I held my breath. Would the combustible situation I had previously overheard arise? Her authority was being challenged, and worse, I was being used as a stick to beat her with by the very boy who had challenged her over completing a poster previously.

'That's right, Neal, and that's what learning is all about – learning with and from other people, and I hope to learn from you in your homework. Mr Creasy tells me you used to be very creative for him when he set homework like this. The thing is, I know you'll be even better for me as you're a year older and wiser and just wait till I show him what you've done for me.'

'Deal, he'll be dead jealous! Just one question, Miss.'

'Yes, Neal, what is it?'

'Can I do a poster?' (Asked in perhaps the most innocent voice I ever heard a fifteen-year-old muster.)

Hearing the whole class collapse laughing I knew all was well, more so when the work was completed and Neal came to show me his work before handing it in. 'Do you think she'll like it?' he asked. Looking at a model, complete with iPod to play dramatic music for the display, I turned all Simon Cowell: 'No, Neal, I don't think she'll like it … she'll love it! Well done!' And of course she did; the work was galleried, the teacher didn't look back (capability was a distant memory), and she gained promotion to become head of department, before leaving to become an assist-

ant head teacher. She is now a deputy head and Neal gained an A* with her!

Different roles = different problems

Whilst Neal's experience may hearten you, it is probably the greatest epiphany I have witnessed. I recognise that, for various reasons, colleagues who undertake Unhomework with their classes may well be challenged. So, as an aide to you, I have tried to consider the varying contexts this discussion may take. I admit I may not have factored in every individual nuance for you, but I believe that there's enough relevance from what's here. (You can contact me if you feel I could be more helpful for your individual circumstances. Please refer to the Twitter account at the end of the book.)

The ITT/NQT – aka 'Why are you trying to run before you can walk?'

Ostensibly this is a tricky one as you do actually have to pass your ITT/NQT year and so it would be ridiculous for me to simply state that you should just 'Go for it!' However, it is in these years (unlike any other time in your professional career) when you have a 'professional/mentor safety net' that I would encourage you to try many new and different things. Clearly, in your ITT year, it isn't 'your class' and so a delicate balance needs to be struck. My simple advice is to refer to DAD (Discuss–Apply–Discuss) so that your mentor understands your thinking and can add their experience to your perspective. Remember, as an ITT it's their class and they have to take over once you've gone. You can experiment and try new things and fail in a constructive way. Remember the words of Thomas Edison: 'I have not failed. I've just found 10,000 ways that won't work.'

If you have sound reasoning and ideas – and hopefully this book has provided numerous examples for you – then start by having a discussion about what you want to do and what you hope to achieve. What will be the success measure, and, crucially, how is it of benefit and relevant? What you are not doing is overtly criticising their current way of doing things. In my experience, the best mentors will support you. In fact, most old hands look forward to learning from new colleagues to keep them 'fresh' – though some teachers, unfortunately, hope for a kind of *Stepford Wives* utopia, where everyone is cloned in their image.

Fair to say, you may well meet a heavy dose of cynicism and scepticism, so be prepared to be able to promote Unhomework based on the expectation of it failing. That's why the 5Rs are so vital. If they are in place you have the foundations for Unhomework. Remember that they apply to you as well as the children, so Relationships and Respect are key, and, as you will discover, Resilience is needed too! A word of caution here: as an ITT you may find the 5Rs are not embedded in your given class or classes, so it would be incredibly brave to attempt

Unhomework without them. If that's the case, resolve to secure them in your own class or classes and perhaps defer for a year, though you can start using some of the elements to build your repertoire in preparation.

The new team member – aka 'We don't do it like that around here'

Potentially the most difficult one (it is for me). You are a successful teacher (your record proves it) and you have moved to a new post in another school. You have left behind a group or two, or even most of the school, where you had them eating out of the palm of your hand. Now you are confronted with the kind of welcome that you might expect if you were a 1970s stand-up comedian at an equal rights convention. Clearly, to your colleagues, you need to establish (or rather prove) yourself. My wisdom tells me that you start from their point of view: what are their likely concerns or misconceptions? Furthermore, unless you've been headhunted to solve problems or it's a new school, the team was functioning well before you arrived (though this may only be true in their own minds) and as a new member your status will be low. You may even discover that you were appointed over a candidate they preferred, possibly one of the established teachers you now need to impress. The reality is that *you* were appointed, not them. That makes all the difference!

In such circumstances, I recommend that MUM and DAD make an appearance as early as possible, preferably within your application form. Certainly during the interview there will always be an opportunity to share something you're particularly proud of or want to expand upon. This is your chance. Now, the risks are that your application letter is rejected, the panel bursts out laughing when you leave the room and that you don't get the job. However, ask yourself: if you believe in it and they are so against it that it costs you your interview, would you want to work there anyway? By making sure you have spoken to the school as early as possible there is the possibility of a 'you have been warned' mentality. But remember that not all of your colleagues will have been involved, so talk to them. Do not, under any circumstances, assume they will understand or accept your way of working or even consider it feasible. Just recall the saying about what happens when you assume!

For your colleagues, establish the understanding that it's a *process*. Ensure that you can tie in your method with the school/department/year group ethos. Show them that you're not quite the maverick they perhaps thought at first. Though there's nothing wrong with being a maverick; as Steve Jobs said, 'The people who are crazy enough to think they can change the world are the ones who do.'

However, there was (unfortunately) only one Steve Jobs, and there is only one you, and you have to be you to the best of your ability. That said, share your ideas with them as early as possible. Explain how things have gone for you previously (the challenges, the successes and the learning) and be prepared for the hackneyed responses of the not-invented-here syndrome, such as, 'But that won't work here/with these kids/for this age group …' Be prepared that they will need to see evidence of it working to believe what you're saying. This is fair enough. Your job is to maintain the dialogue that keeps them informed. It's worth discussing the children as they will know them better than you – and listen to what they say!

The established colleague – aka 'Why are you now doing it like that?'

The benefit for you if you are this teacher is that you have the foothold in the department, team or school that the colleagues above do not enjoy. However, a new approach from you will still be viewed with suspicion as you will be 'breaking the mould'. Here my advice is simple: use the relationships and respect you have established with your colleagues over your time at the school and discuss your thoughts with them. Maybe even give them a copy of this book.

The other advantage you have is the potential to undertake this as action research. This would give you credence with colleagues and allow you to have facts as well as feedback from the children, all the while honing your approach to Unhomework. The clear danger here is that your colleagues, or even friends, may be afraid that this may translate to a potential change in their practice. To minimise resistance, stay open and instigate discussions and observation. Be prepared to share how the children are doing, and yes, including where it goes wrong. The wry, sage admission over a pint (or coffee, if you prefer) that, 'It didn't quite work with Wayne or Roxanne,' will bring knowing smiles, perhaps an, 'I told you so,' but fundamentally it will mean a conversation occurs.

The leader – aka 'Well, it's easy for you, isn't it!'

The irony here is th I have heard this accusation levelled at everyone from a head teacher to an NQT. The apparent reasons vary as to why it's easier for one person with the children than another; it usually has to do with authority or perception of the colleagues' subjects. It has amused me over the years to find that it's supposedly easier for PE, art, drama and music teachers. I think the unspoken prejudice relates to them not being deemed 'proper' subjects. And before you send lots of complaints or abuse, I remind you that I say this as a trained PE teacher! Though my favourite response actually came from an NQT, only two weeks into his time at the school (and who is now an assistant head). Apparently it's still 'easy' for him:

Colleague: Of course, it's easy for you as a PE teacher.

NQT: Really?

Colleague: The fact is that you're an NQT too.

NQT: I don't get it.

Colleague: Well the kids love your subject, and the fact you're not a 'proper teacher' yet makes it easier for you too.

NQT (*showing great restraint from thumping said person*): I still don't get it!

Colleague: Well the difference between your lessons and mine is that yours are like Disneyland and mine are not.[1]

NQT: What, you mean the kids want to come to my lessons and they don't want to come to yours?

This left the colleague speechless (a rare treat for the rest of us) and was how the NQT earned the moniker 'Walt' from that day on, to the extent that some people didn't actually know his real name until his leaving speech when the head teacher used it – and for some people that caused confusion as they didn't know who was being spoken about!

Anyway, the twofold danger for the leader if they decide to pursue Unhomework is that (a) colleagues will expect it to become whole school policy (not that that would be such a problem, but the best policy would be five words long: 'We do not set homework'), or (b) it is dismissed as only working due to their specific role or status in the

---

1 Of course, this comment was made in the 'traditional' way, not having seen the NQT teach or even been in the same department, but you know how it is with some colleagues!

school. The other unfortunate danger with a leader adopting Unhomework is that the expectant group want to see it fail, to be able to retort, 'Well, if they can't make it work …' The honest truth here is that something of this kind will always happen in an organisation – it's human nature. Progress comes when you believe in yourself, maintain your resilience, dust yourself off, reflect as to why it didn't work (what did you do wrong?) and have another go once you have reflected on how to do it better.

The key factor about being a leader and teaching is the ability to disassociate the two, especially for the children. They are not guinea pigs for an Unhomework experiment that may lead to a potential whole school doctrine, nor are the staff going to match your successes, at least at first. There may be a desire to try and 'get this to work' regardless during INSET days – that won't help the teachers, the children or you! Be yourself, and enjoy using a method that you believe in and subscribe to, and which, hopefully, you have used before. This is no different from any other teaching tool at your disposal. Engage with colleagues in genuine discussion about the merits of Unhomework. Avoid being too evangelical about it and, most importantly, have fun developing your Unhomework style. As the Olympic alpine ski racer Bode Miller says, 'Fun is the source of all joy.' (And he should know!)

Ultimately, when promoting Unhomework it will be the children who are your greatest advocates. This will show that they not only enjoy the process in your class but actually understand it! Then, irrespective of their current teachers' methods and philosophies, they will Unhomework for themselves (as shown by Neal's initial conversation above). That, for me, is the greatest testimony to the notion that children lead their own learning. No, you won't have great acclaim, but is that why you're doing it? Of course not! The byproducts of Unhomework will be the stolen moments: a discussion at break or lunchtime, or a sharing of some work they have done and are proud of. That is the best reward possible. Trust me, it's happened to me many times!

Their questions, your answers

Ideally, if things have gone as I would hope, then your preparatory conversations with colleagues will ensure that they have a basic understanding of, and a healthy interest in, promoting Unhomework. However, for some people this nirvana will not exist.

So in that spirit, the following responses provide some way to justify your approach and persuade others. You can add these to your armoury for the professional learning conversations you are going to have. There should be enough here to adapt your response to a range of negative statements which might be put forward.

Question: How will this help them pass their exams?

Answers:

+ Aren't we about more than just that?

+ By knowing how they learn best they'll be more effective come exam time.

+ It will broaden their horizons for thinking and working differently.

+ It will develop skills to complement their exam successes.

+ It will help them at that moment in the exams when they have to rely on themselves, when they don't know what to do. This way they won't panic, as they'll have had the experience before.

Question: So what are you doing if they set the work?

Answers:

+ (Adopting the appropriate sarcastic tone) Clearly not very much! (It depends on who this is said to – probably not best to any of the SLT. When I tried this once it didn't go down well!)

- Trying to be the 'guide on the side', not the 'sage on the stage'.

- Supporting them to make sure it's still purposeful and challenging.

- Preparing lessons to build on their work.

Question: How do you know it's their own work? (This is my favourite one!)

Answers:

- How do we ever know that?

- I trust them; the work is built on the 5Rs … (which I then explain).

- If it's not, who ultimately loses out?

Question: What if the work isn't up to standard?

Answers:

- They have set the criteria, it's up to them.

- We discuss it; there could be a reason.

- Their learning partner will soon tell me when they mark it!

- It's reflected in my marking, after being marked by themselves and their peers.

- It can always be redone – if that's what we decide.

Question: If they're doing all this, aren't you telling them they don't need you?

Answers:

- I hope so!

- Not at all … It's the guide/sage role …

- Have you read Ian Gilbert's *Why Do I Need a Teacher When I've Got Google?* ?

- Why would you think that?

Question: But is this covered in the homework policy?

Answers:

+ What does the policy actually say then? (This often stumps them!)

+ The policy requires … and Unhomework meets this by …

+ Homework is set, marked, commented on and followed up. So what about that isn't in the policy?

+ It's because of the policy that I can do this. (Remember, sometimes colleagues will just be scared and want permission to take a different route.)

+ It is; let's look together at it and you can try this out too – I know you'd love it.

Using children as convincers

Ultimately, the children will be your greatest asset for delivering Unhomework to a wider audience. You need to ensure that other colleagues can see that the children have bought into the process and have understood it, if you are going to be able to expound its benefits to them. As I have said before, you will know that Unhomework is truly part of the child's psyche when they carry out Unhomework without you, even when they are with a colleague who does not use these methods in their lessons with them. However, as parents know, pester power is a strong force and children who show that they want to take command over their learning will often be welcomed. Whilst there might be an initial air of suspicion, it will be your job to cement the Unhomework philosophy into the children and allow them to have a script to engage in effective dialogue with other teachers.

As Neal showed above, despite his protestations being ignored he still completed his own work, as well as the poster, which showed his teacher that he wanted to work and was prepared to give more time to the subject. This, applied across staff and allied to your conversations, will move Unhomework forward within your school. It is because children are likely to challenge the status quo and seek to use Unhomework that it cannot be some form of conspiracy against the system between you and them whilst you teach them. If you haven't spoken to colleagues, or at least let it be known what you are doing, the children will simply appear noncompliant and awkward. Remember, these children will have already helped you convince sceptical parents, so they will be great assets to do the same with staff.

The Magnificent Seven ride again!

Here are my seven favourite comments/questions about Unhomework over the years. These serve to remind me of the truth of what Shirley Whitehouse once told me: 'Never be surprised by the capacity other teachers, more than the kids, have to scare the shit out of you!'

7   'Can you repeat that again? I've got to take notes; no one will believe me when I tell them!'

6   'But how do you cope if you don't set the homework at the start of the lesson?' (Showing Dustin Hoffman's *Rain Man* exists in England too!)

5   'And how do you expect employers to thank you, getting children to think for themselves?' (Yes, this was really said in the twenty-first century, not Victorian England!)

4   'Well, they won't do that in my class, they'll do what they're told.' (Unsurprising and common.)

3   'What do you want them to think for themselves for?'

2   'Whatever next, let's get them to teach as well?' (I had to point out that I do that too!)

1   'So, you actually *trust* them?' (With the emphasis on trust!)

This last comment was delivered by a colleague who also came up with the classic, 'Well you won't need that in my lesson will you?' after she had asked the children why they had water bottles on their desks and they had replied that it was to stop their brains dehydrating so they could think better when learning! How they (or I for that matter) managed not to laugh out loud, I do not know.

CHAPTER FIVE
DEVELOPING UNHOMEWORK ON A WIDER CANVAS

In this together

Now that you have seen some of the benefits of Unhomework and have decided to undertake Unhomework for yourself, you may also want others to be similarly inspired to introduce it into their practice for themselves. It can feel quite exhilarating to be conspiratorial with the children you teach; that between you, you know you are doing things differently from other teachers in other classes. You know that the relationships you have developed thanks to your classroom environment, secured by the 5Rs, have allowed Unhomework to thrive. The children love to feel this difference and enjoy having a feeling of uniqueness; aware they are benefitting but almost wanting to keep that experience for themselves. For you as the professional, this feeling is more likely to have been derived from not wanting to be ridiculed or judged for your way of working. But if you truly believe in Unhomework as a philosophy and not just as a process or a 'teaching app', then you will want this to be painted on a broader canvas.

Once you have worked through the structure outlined in previous chapters, you will witness the progression and development of the children. The quality of the work they produce of their own volition and their increased confidence will delight you and encourage you to go further. You will have seen that despite doubts (and doubters), children even as young as eight can set their own work and criteria for marking and can self- and peer-assess sensibly. Added to that, I know that you will begin to have the great experience of being challenged by your class as their creativity and ingenuity sparks you further and pushes you to try to keep pace with them, trying to meet their needs. Here is an example I experienced recently …

Year 5 Science lesson

Wednesday: Lesson on safety in the lab

The class's task is to provide evidence that they understand how to be safe (the scheme's homework is to complete a poster). Having taught half of the children in Year 4 last year I decided to go with Unhomework for the first homework, getting them to suggest ideas for completion to support their peers in how Unhomework is conducted, but imposed the deadline myself of the following Monday.

Monday: Hand in homework, self- and peer-assess

Of the entire class, only two children completed a poster – one of which was a poster of unsafe things occurring which had to be spotted. The other work included poems, leaflets, cartoons, spot the differences and the creation of a mad professor called Doctor Don't and his sensible twin Doctor Do, who explain the rules. There was even a pastiche of the YouTube video 'Dumb Ways to Die',[1] called 'Dumb Ways to Die in the Science Lab', written, sung and videoed by two of the children. An absolute gem of an idea came from one boy who, in his book, had designed a dice-based board game where safe and unsafe practices made up the board and involved moving forwards or backwards depending on what you landed on! This was even more special to me as I

---

1 http://www.youtube.com/watch?v=IJNR2EpS0jw

hadn't taught him the previous year, so he had clearly understood Unhomework immediately and been prepared to go for it.

Wednesday: Teacher feedback on homework

After praising the class for great efforts (which they were happy to modestly compare to their peers in other classes who had only completed a poster!), I ran a homework lottery ready for the next work. With three winners selected, the following happened:

MC: So this week …

Child 1: Mr Creasy, we were talking, can we do a board like Jake designed?

MC: If you wish.

Child 2: We thought that we could really show what we learned that way and, no offence, Jake, as your game was great, you could do it too as we can make them, not just draw them out.

Jake: I wanted to do that anyway, but Mum said to do it in my book.

MC: Okay, are you happy with that then?

The class consensus was that they were more than happy – it was clear it was a conspiracy!

Child 3 (*lottery winner*): But I don't have to miss out, do I? I want to do this!

MC: You won the lottery, so the point is you choose whether to do the work or not.

Child 3: Great!

MC: Now that's settled, today …

Child 2: Sorry, Mr Creasy, we had another idea.

MC: Don't be sorry, what was it?

Child 1: We thought we could not only design and make the games but we could then play them with Year 3, so we can teach them about safety in a fun way – it's never too early to learn, you know!

Child 2: Especially as two of their classes are next to the lab and they're going to see us with Bunsen burners, chemicals and stuff.

Child 1: And it will also teach them about taking turns, playing fairly and getting along, which Year 3 need as there's a lot of new children, you know.

MC: I had noticed. That sounds like a great idea, I can speak to the teachers.

Child 1: It's okay, we already have – we knew you'd agree to this homework!

At break, I thought it best to check with the Year 3 staff and, indeed, they had been approached. One of them told me that one of my class had summed up the idea as, 'We're going to do a homework in science based on Jake's game and wanted to play them with Year 3 to teach them what we know. Is that okay? We have science on a Monday and a double lesson on a Wednesday.' When my colleague said that she'd check with the other teachers and their timetables then liaise with me, she laughed when she was told, 'Hmm okay, but don't do it before our lesson on Wednesday. Mr Creasy doesn't know that he's doing that yet!'

Monday: Games brought in

Planned lesson (partially) forgotten, we play the safety games to assess them and give feedback to ensure when the children go to the three Year 3 classes they work as they want them to.

All in all this was a great example, not only of Unhomework but also of the 5Rs in action, especially the strength of the relationships with the, 'No offence, Jake ...' comment, where praise for his idea led to constructive feedback and group development – as well as Jake's mum learning to leave the Unhomework to him because he had a great idea!

So, having previously explained and outlined your philosophy to your colleagues about what you intend to achieve through Unhomework, the ripple effect should be tangible as the children develop their independence and it is witnessed by other staff. This cannot be achieved by seclusion in your own room, marvelling at what your children achieve but not letting others share in it – becoming a kind of educational Gollum!

Spreading the word

Thanks to your successes and increased confidence with deploying Unhomework, and having convinced your colleagues that this philosophy has derived a way of working that is of greater benefit for the children than traditional homework, the time will come when Unhomework can be spread further. Be under no illusion that staff and parents will be watching you and monitoring the methods used, in order to witness the impact of Unhomework – often jealously wishing they could do it too. This is the tack to take when supporting them in doing so. You will have actual experience to fall back on, with children they know. This will get you beyond the usual initial scepticism regarding the relative ability of the children to do it.

From the staff's own observations, as well as the feedback and positive comments from both the children and their parents, their interest will have been sparked. Children they know, perhaps even better than you, will have a different demeanour and will be able to explain what has happened and how they feel about it. This is why the DAD model and MUM process are so important, as they allow for the articulation of Unhomework, not just a random mumbling about not really doing homework, or it being homework but different! This means that, at some point, perhaps even as early as by Christmas, those around you will show greater interest in wanting to employ this method for themselves.

This is an important moment in the evolution of Unhomework, for upon your advice and support will hang the future success of Unhomework in your school. Yes, it may be nice to be known as the one person doing something different, accepting the plaudits and brickbats for your philosophy, but if it is a true philosophy then surely you'd like others to take up the challenge! It is far too simplistic to say, 'Just read this book,' and send them on their way. Hopefully at some point in prior dialogue you will have mentioned this book to them, but the point is they aren't doing Unhomework! There will be some form of block, often self-imposed, perhaps even prejudicial, as to why they or their classes cannot succeed with this manner of working. Think of the experiences and valid reasons stated above that Neal's teacher had as to why Unhomework was anathema to her initially. Similarly, it is too risky to expect Unhomework to work for your colleagues just because it does for you. As others raise their interest, you must remember that you have worked hard for your success, so do not brush it off as 'just one of those things'. What you have achieved wasn't simply done, and if you explain it as such you not only do a disservice to your hard work but also implicitly tell colleagues that you are able to do something they cannot.

Below I outline how I have seen Unhomework implemented on a wider scale, though I do not claim these are the only ways to achieve this success; I am sure colleagues who have implemented their own developments in learning and teaching will have their own ways of securing success on a larger scale. However, the fundamental point is to recall the 5Rs, the DAD Model and the MUM process – ensure that your colleagues appreciate these and secure them first. If your success has inspired others they will only have had an overview and seen your achievement, not knowing the minutiae of detail that has gone into securing it. I compare it to the student teacher coming into a class midway through the year and seeing the children eating out of the palm of the teacher's hand, then thinking they will never have such ease and aplomb in a classroom. Hard as it may be, remember the work you have put into achieving that apparent ease that others now see. It is actually this which has inspired them to seek out your way of working with the children, as this has provided the fruits of your labour. If you engage in professional modesty that will only serve you in brushing off compliments. If you agree that yes, you do make it look easy, that will only increase the chances that their attempts will fail or flounder – sometimes before they even get off the ground.

Unhomework across a department

Ideally, this is how Unhomework can spread further – be it in a year group, subject department or faculty – as you receive the time and support from your colleagues to develop the process. These colleagues will be the ones you spoke to initially and possibly had to convince that your philosophy was sound. They will have observed you implement Unhomework in your class(es) as they continued in their traditional way of setting homework. They have had the best opportunity to see how things work in your room compared to theirs and to trust you in implementing it with your class(es), regardless of how they are working with theirs. It is entirely possible that your subject leader has decided to join you in the Unhomework mission and it was a department-wide initiative from the off.

So, without wishing to repeat the advice about dealing with sceptics, I suggest the following simple steps:

1 Collect feedback from the children about Unhomework – positive and negative.

2 Record the types of work the children produce – copy or photograph it. This is also useful to ensure that they aren't always completing the same type of work (Remember what Picasso said: 'I am always doing that which I cannot do, in order that I may learn how to do it'.)

3 Create an Unhomework gallery in your room to show off the work.

4 Invite the department leader to come into your lessons to witness Unhomework and discuss it with the children.

5   Discuss with the department leader their views and observations.

6   Secure time at a department meeting – often pressured, but as every meeting should have time given over to learning and teaching (if not, what's it for?), do use this opportunity. Agree with the department leader that everyone will trial this. Don't go to the meeting to have a discussion – you know it works, you're there to help your colleagues implement it.

7   Suggest to the department leader that as Unhomework is founded on the 5Rs, perhaps a discussion on classroom philosophy might be useful. This should ease the burden on you and also prevent you from (inadvertently) telling everyone how great you are and that if only their rooms had your atmosphere the world would be a better place.[2]

8   Having secured the time, create a simple step-by-step guide – I have tended to use Genesis (The Bible, not Phil Collins's band) as a model. 'In the beginning …'

9   Hold the meeting in your room to evidence the children's work.

10 Discuss fears using the department leader for support, as they've witnessed it too.

11 Agree how it will be phased in; perhaps a year group or subject at a time as people build confidence.

12 Use the key markers for early Unhomework development as outlined in this book.

13 Send a departmental communiqué home to all parents so that they know what is going on and why.

---

2   I have to admit that was my approach once, not that I realised it at the time – I thought it was all so obvious! Now, with hindsight and experience, I see my mistakes and how insecure it made other people feel. It wasn't a pretty meeting and so the department took a full year to implement Unhomework fully and effectively. When

---

we did, it worked brilliantly, as my colleagues were forgiving, but it was a good example of not considering the views and perceptions of others when you are blinded by enthusiasm.

14 Establish a rolling programme of support. Using your department blog or the virtual learning environment (VLE) is a great idea, as children can share in the experience. (If you don't have a department blog, www.edmodo.com is a great site for allowing children to share work and converse safely about learning. Put simply, it's an educational Facebook which the teacher controls and is private to your class and the school.)

15 Follow up the progress in future meetings, developing the roll-out over a sensible, but not sluggish, time frame so that everyone is benefitting.

Whole school Unhomework

Potentially this can be trickier, as this could be seen as challenging the authority of the leaders, and, depending on your position in the school hierarchy, self-promotion for future gain. Also, given that there is going to be someone in charge of learning and teaching on your SLT, it would be a good idea if they have invested in the idea early on, so they need to be one of the first conversations you have when initiating Unhomework. It is likely that your department will have a member of the SLT in it and they can be a useful ally in supporting any whole school development, as they will have witnessed first-hand how the process works and the impact it has on the children.

Some words of caution:

+ Unless you are an SLT member, you will probably not be aware of the wrangling and egos of the team that lead the school. Whatever you think you know thanks to staffroom or corridor observations will not even be the half of it, believe me. It is important, therefore, to make sure you discuss what is going on with several members of the team, preferably all of them, but most of all the head teacher. Opportunities for one-upmanship and comments of, 'What? You didn't know?' are seldom wasted in an SLT, especially if the ignorant party is in charge of learning and teaching or there is enmity between the person you told and another. This will clearly affect your chances of securing the broadest canvas possible, as involving only a few people from the SLT will almost certainly set the others against it automatically. This is usually more likely if one of those told is not the head teacher, who then finds out something is going on in their school through a casual comment or SLT bickering.

+ If you want Unhomework to be broader, be prepared to let go of it. Realise that you may find your work is taken on by others – sometimes promoted as their own. Now that is fine – unless you also have a megalomaniacal ego and see

Unhomework as your path to glory, promotion and world domination! However, it is most important to ensure the integrity of the philosophy and make certain that if someone else is delivering it then you are part of the process of delivery, be it in a meeting or INSET; even simply through sharing your experience and knowledge, or being prepared to be a learning buddy for others.

Having said all of that, securing whole school Unhomework can prove extremely easy, given the right circumstances. The whole school process should be very similar to that of the department. Reread the bullet points above and just substitute SLT for subject leader and staff meeting or INSET for department meeting to see how it works. The most important factor, which is worth repeating, is ensuring the classroom climate is correct for Unhomework: the 5Rs. This is the basis from which you will build. It may be scary for some staff as it could lead to a whole school review of philosophy and ethos. However, this should be seen as liberating.

Once the philosophy and ethos are secure, whether that has occurred (preferably) in the same meeting or perhaps teed up previously, the staff meeting can build on this for Unhomework to be developed across the school.

Maintaining support

The next decisive element is the ongoing support needed to maintain momentum. Whoever you are – and as much as you may want to – you will not be able to support every member of staff, nor will they all be delivering in a classroom in the way you do. Trying to make that happen will be futile. This is where you need to lean on your department and put in place the following support mechanisms:

+ Delivery at staff meeting, with timetable for the roll-out. Do not try to deliver this single handedly, use your department colleagues to aid presentation, lead and support group work and even

provide testimonials about how Unhomework has worked for them. This will allow other elements of the roll-out to go smoothly as you are not seen to be saying 'Do it like me, I'm great!'[3]

+ Establish support groups for staff teams. Cross-department works best here as it will break down barriers, encourage people to work outside their usual group and also add a dimension to departments as they witness what others are doing.

+ Each support group should have an Unhomework champion, drawn from your department,

---

3 If the head teacher does not attend staff meetings, insist they do for this one – if they have a prior arrangement, either rearrange the staff meeting or delay Unhomework's introduction. When a new idea is launched there is nothing more off-putting for staff than when the head teacher or several SLT are absent. Not only does it tell colleagues their view of the importance of your initiative, it also says a lot about the impetus behind it and the likely follow-up. Ian Gilbert produced a helpful guide through Independent Thinking, which was based on testimonies from their associates, that highlights behaviours to avoid for anyone if Unhomework is to be successfully launched: http://www.independentthinking.com/Cool+Stuff/Handouts/429.aspx (registration required).

who will (hopefully) have been part of the stepwise change process. They will have experienced the feelings others will likely have and will be best placed to support them – you can't do it all!

+ Departments feed back to each other from their experiences with their classes and from what they've learnt from working with colleagues beyond their department.

+ Follow-up in the next staff meeting, led by the champions. Involve feedback from the pastoral team and non-teaching staff, especially those not in classrooms, on what differences they have seen.

+ Departments create their own gallery of work, with explanations by the children (this may need some work if videos, songs, etc. are produced – but that's your challenge).

Once Unhomework has received its wider audience, there is the huge temptation to switch off and simply cede control to individual staff. However, each department will need to monitor the work being produced by the children. This is probably best done through department reviews or simply through meetings. Here is where children's champions – or the school council – can be used: to provide input and feedback. The children will be able to talk about standards across the school: are teachers fulfilling the brief? Are they allowing truly independent work? How are they finding it? Squaring that circle and including the children is the best way to secure Unhomework across your school.

Cross phase/transition work

I would like to believe that this is easy. Surely if all primary schools deployed Unhomework from Year 4 upwards, then secondary schools would simply follow suit and children could start Year 7 with teachers knowing they were capable and so allowing them to be creative and individual. However, that is not the case. Given that primary schools will invariably supply several secondaries, and that secondary schools will draw from numerous primaries, each sector is reliant upon the other if they have introduced Unhomework already. For this reason, I will deal with each possibility separately, outlining how to develop a more cohesive approach for the children who will move upwards through education. The truth is, it's the children who cope best with these differences; not only the changing demands and expectations, but also up to fifteen versions of them from different teachers. As observed before, what a shame we pay so little respect to their individuality as learners and yet expect them to respect the differences of all their teachers!

Primary

If you work in the primary sector and have introduced Unhomework, it would be great to support your secondary colleagues and show how responsible your learners are. This would give them a flying start to secondary school life and not make the children feel they are starting from scratch. In reality, you know that is not always the case – understandably, given the diversity of primary schools a secondary will work with and the different number of children they will take from each. I used to have the role of primary transition coordinator for my Luton school, which gave me twenty-six primaries to work with, providing between one and thirty-six children each; I'm sure secondary colleagues will have comparable experience. This does not mean that primaries have it any easier, for they will, in turn, also work with a diverse range of secondary schools – each with unique expectations.

Your role is to showcase your children's work and provide evidence of how they work. When completing Unhomework, teach your children how to create a portfolio and support them in providing diverse examples of their talents, with self-assessment and commentaries on the work and their efforts too. An idea I have used in the past is to get the children to show their work cross-referenced against the PLTS, and this has shown their new teachers how they have worked.

I would also suggest the common practice of an extended project in the summer term – after SATs is an ideal time – to develop transition work with your secondary colleagues. Using Mission: Homework (see Appendix 2) to complement the project will allow secondary colleagues to provide insight into what they'd like to see from the children when they arrive in September. This will also give an opportunity for some completion over the holidays so that children can include holidays, days out and interests as part of their Unhomework to take to secondary school. You can encourage them by reinforcing the idea of a first impression being important, as well as this project providing a showcase for everything they have learnt at primary school.

Secondary

It can also be tricky for secondary staff to work with a diverse range of primary schools, just as primaries have diverse secondaries to work with. Ideally, a localised hub of secondaries could coordinate similar requests from their primaries to ease their workload and allow all children to collaborate at primary school, before presenting their own work in September. It might be an ideal, but really, what's stopping you doing this? Imagine if all secondaries took this on, launched a transition project with their primary colleagues and allowed all the children to feel a sense of achievement and collegiality before they left primary school. This would mean that when the new intake arrived, there would already be a commonality for all children and ample speaking and listening opportunities to allow them to engage with each other beyond their immediate friendship groups. The added bonus is that it will tell you a lot about who does what and how the work is completed.

If you are the secondary school who is championing Unhomework, the problem is how to engage with your primary colleagues without it sounding like a dictated set of demands, or coming across as though you know best for the children they have known and guided for over seven years in many cases. In the first instance, work with your largest feeder primary school(s) in establishing a transition project so the majority of your Year 7s have the desired commonality. This is a more realistic starting point, probably necessitating work with no more than three to five schools. Admittedly, this will mean that some of the new intake will not have completed this transition work when they arrive in September, but if you set the first two weeks' homework as completing any remaining elements of the transition project work, this is solved. It will not only include the new children, but have the added bonus of providing easy display work for the imminent open evening at the end of September or early October.

In my experience, the best advice for the secondary school transfer is not to presume what the children, or staff for that matter, at a primary *cannot* do, but rather to trust them as professional colleagues whose work you will be continuing and developing. Too often children are expected to be at a certain place, often to fit the scheme of work designed by the secondary school, regardless of the fact they are often well beyond this. A recent conversation I had proves this (even though I had hoped these conversations were a thing of the past):

MC: When do you set in maths?

Teacher: When they come in, in Year 7; we have a look at them for a bit then decide.

MC: What are you looking at?

Teacher: How good they are at maths.

MC: Why don't you use their national curriculum levels?

Teacher: Well, they're not always accurate; they're for primary schools and so different to a secondary.

MC: Really, how so?

Teacher: Well, er, well they're teacher assessed as well.

MC: But they aren't the national curriculum levels are they?

Teacher: No, but they make a difference.

MC: How? I thought you would have two sets of information for your children – the national curriculum level and teacher assessment – and could set adequately from there?

Teacher: Wow, you seem to know your stuff! No one usually goes into this much depth. It's just how we do it.

MC: Okay.

Teacher: Really?

MC: No, but if that's what you do with no real reason, I can't change it.

Teacher: Well …

MC: I'm sorry to interrupt, but to save you further embarrassment, I am a teacher, have taught in secondary school and currently teach in a primary school, so I know there's no reason not to set immediately.

Teacher: Oh … I wondered, as you knew what you were talking about.

This was on an open evening tour of a local school, which my daughter won't be attending!

I am hopeful that if you have undertaken Unhomework you really are more enlightened than this secondary colleague. If so, engage with the primary schools and discuss potential projects in the summer the year before transfer so that everyone has the opportunity to plan together. Secondary schools do plan transitions, though this is not always communicated adequately, apart from induction days in the summer term. My advice is to get together one summer to plan the project for the next year – consider holding it in the primary school; do not assume that they should come to the secondary.

Follow up the initial planning at regular intervals with liaison between those responsible for Years 6 and 7. Include the teachers and also the school council, ideally using some of your current Year 7 so they can provide first-hand experience of the transition. Perhaps include them in the project design, too, so that they can act as ambassadors to children who will know them and look up to them.

The last part of the transition jigsaw does not come in the summer term when the work is being completed, or even in September when it is handed in. No, the final element is to invite the primary school teachers into your school to see the showcase of your work, with their former children showing it off to them. Added to this, they do not attend alone, but bring the current Year 6 to see what happens between your two schools to start the link as early as possible. Actually, this isn't the final part of the process

– that comes in your evaluation of the project, seeing how successful Unhomework was, including the views of staff and children and using it to design the next project.[4]

---

4 Note for primary colleagues: if and when secondary colleagues do come to visit (or parents for parents' evenings), get out some suitably sized chairs. It's embarrassing and unprofessional to expect everyone to sit on the chairs designed for a five-year-old. If that's not possible, book the staffroom and meet in there. Otherwise, the wrong tone is set and secondary colleagues will wonder why they came to you, rather than stay and invite you to them!

CHAPTER SIX
MY FAVOURITE UNHOMEWORKS

Now that you have reached an understanding and appreciation of Unhomework, this chapter provides some examples of how you can get work from your children without really setting it. I have separated the examples into the two phases of education, as well as indicating the year group who provided it. Remember that none of this was secured in isolation, so there are pointers to how and where the work I refer to fitted in with the learning the children were undertaking at the time.

Examples from primary school children

Cake Club

In the 2012 academic year, possibly my favourite Unhomework was created – though my expanding waistline should force me not to enjoy it! I was teaching maths with the Year 4 upper set. I had just started to introduce Unhomework to them and so the children were given the following task:

TV Homework – Great British Bake Off vs Grand Designs

Either develop your skills with weights, measures and time by baking a cake, or develop your shape, length and area skills by redesigning your bedroom.

The enthusiasm was exceptional and the children immediately discussed how they could develop the work even further. This led to these two amazing examples: Harriet went a step further than designing her bedroom and actually came in with a scale model of how she would like her room to look, with dimensions measured and recorded on the outside of the box. This was delivered the very day after the work was set and allowed me to reiterate the fact that handing in work early was only acceptable if it was of a high quality. This was.

Seeing Harriet's model sparked an interest in Emma, who frantically made notes in her planner but would not let me see what she had written. On the day the homework was due in I saw what she had done. She had created a gingerbread model of her dream bedroom, combining both homework tasks, which she called her Great British Grand Design!

However, this ingenuity and the cakes that other children brought in (obviously as the teacher I had to taste the cakes to mark the homework properly) led to the following exchange between James and me:

James: Mr Creasy, can we do that homework again?

MC: Well, I'm not going to set it. It's up to you. Why?

James: I love baking and wish I'd made a cake now, seeing these. I'm not being rude, but you'd really love my cake!

MC: I do love these, James, but I'm always happy to try another cake.

James: Or four!

MC: Thank you!

James: I know! Why don't we have a class cake club? That way we can always have cake and everyone who isn't in our maths class can join in too!

MC: How would that work?

James: Er, hmm, I don't know yet – I'll come back to you after break.

After break, despite my best efforts to get ready for English …

James: Mr Creasy, I've got it.

MC: Have you? Okay, everyone listen.

James: Right, it's simple. The rules are: 1) You don't have to take part but if you do, your parents have to agree; 2) *You* have to make the cake. No cheating and getting parents to do it – they can help, but not do it; 3) No shop-bought cakes, what's the point? We choose two people at random each week, how's that sound?

MC: Great, but 4) No nuts.

James: Oh yeah, that – we don't want to kill anyone, do we?

MC: No, of course not (*slight cough*).

And from that, cake club was born and ran the whole year!

Talking and dressing Chinese

I had created a restaurant project for a class where the children, in randomly selected groups, had to design a restaurant for the type of food they were allocated – again at random. The groups had to create menus, posters, TV and radio adverts and shop designs. The aim was to have a truly cross-curricular project that allowed the children to select their areas of interest and expertise as well as develop those in which they were not so strong.

Believing that the children should lead the work, I assented when by lunchtime of the project day the children were asking if they could have another day to work on it. I pointed out that the next day's learning would have to be recovered somewhere. 'We'll give up Golden Time!'[1] came a cry in unison. Clearly they'd discussed this!

When I came in the next morning I was impressed, though not surprised, to see how much work the children had completed overnight, without being told to – though funnily enough each group was disappointed that their cunning plan to get ahead had been similarly considered by the other children. However, I was astonished by the group creating a Chinese restaurant, The Great Wok of China. One of the girls had taken it upon herself to translate their

---

1 Golden Time is the part of the week in our curriculum for up to Year 4 when the children have the freedom to 'play' in the classroom: Lego, drawing, board games, etc. It happens once a week, usually on a Friday afternoon.

entire menu into Mandarin. Milly told me that she had spent two hours on the translation, but it was worth it because when she got older she intended to be an entrepreneur and would need to learn Mandarin to do business globally (she was only 9 years old!)

As I was digesting this I saw Alana, another girl from the Chinese restaurant group, carrying a large bag over a hanger and was curious to see what she had. She lifted the bag to reveal a full-size uniform for the restaurant staff, made out of linen and decorated with different coloured fabrics she had stuck on; she had also done some stitching and sewn on some beads. I asked her how she had created this, a bit nervous about the possible expense, but she told me her mum had some spare material and she had used that. 'Anyway, Mr Creasy, I'm going to be a dress designer when I'm older so it's all good practice, you know. In fact, you'll hear my name for designing a wedding dress for the royal family one day.'

As you may have guessed, The Great Wok of China was the winning restaurant, as voted for by the other children. However, the interesting element to this project came after the weekend when, despite it not counting towards the project, children brought in other translated menus and uniforms, as well as having made TV adverts on iPods, recorded radio adverts, made models of the restaurants and made some of the menu for the class to sample! When asked why they had done this, the best response came from Connor: 'I didn't know what I could do until I saw others doing it – they inspired me.'

Bored game

In the academic year 2010, my first in a primary school, I decided to get the children to demonstrate their learning from our rainforest topic by creating a game which would link to our English work of writing instructions. The children set about designing a board game. They were allowed to select their partners, and, after an initial discussion about types of games and what makes a game successful, the children worked towards their deadline of a fortnight. This could include lesson time and work at home, too, if they felt it needed it. However, one of the children, Jake, was struggling for ideas. He had asked if he could work by himself, which had disappointed the others because he was popular, but his reasoning was that he couldn't cope with so many people wanting to work with him!

This led to a dilemma: the whole purpose of the project was not only to collaborate but to create the game independently of me to show their learning. However, how could I just sit and watch, letting Jake struggle? I sat with him as he flicked through his topic book looking for inspiration. The following conversation happened:

MC: So what are you thinking about?

Jake: My problem is I know all the stuff, it's just how to make it interesting.

MC: How do you mean?

Jake: Well, I listened to everyone and I can see what they're all doing, but I want to be different.

MC: Well …

Jake: I don't want you to tell me, I know the PLTS objective for me is to be a self-manager.

MC: No. My only thought is: think about you, not everyone else.

Walking off, I saw Jake stop flicking and consider my advice. I knew what I thought he should do, but he had to see it for himself or it'd be pointless. For the rest of the lesson he sat there making notes and writing some questions, but I knew he was just filling time until inspiration hit. As a teacher, clearly this was a risk. There is the perception that every child must be engaged for every minute of every lesson. However, for me to tell him how to fulfil this task would mean he had failed the most important objective: to develop his skills and solve the problem for himself. Also, with a fortnight to work with, I felt one lesson could be forsaken, and I trusted him to consider the project overnight.

The next morning, as I arrived in school at 8:05, Jake was already at the classroom door, a huge grin on his face.

Jake: I've got it, Mr Creasy!

MC: Really, and at 8 o'clock in the morning!

Jake: No, my project – I thought about it and worked it out during dinner!

MC: Okay, so what are you thinking?

Jake: Well, I have one question first. Does it have to be a board game?

MC: What are John and Kal doing?

Jake: Designing Top Trumps. Oh, YES!

MC: Is that good news then?

Jake: Yes, I'm going to design a game to be played on a computer. You know I have my own website? Well (*before I could answer*), I'm planning to write a game, put it on my site, then the children answer the questions and submit them and the computer marks it for them. How's that?

MC: (*Being deliberately provocative*) Why not just write some question and answer cards?

Jake: (*Incredulous*) Where's the challenge or fun in that?

MC: Okay, if you're sure. What do you need from me?

Jake: Hmm, no offence, but nothing – I need to see Mr S for some programming advice, but I don't think you're up to it.

MC: No, you're probably right, but can I ask a favour? Can you explain to me how you write the program for the game – as it's not my area of expertise?

Suffice to say the game was delivered and the children loved it. Jake completed the game in lesson time and in ICT. The other children did not complain that he got to use a laptop when they didn't, or that he had special privileges to access sites usually blocked to children. After the children played the game, Jake showed us a PowerPoint to explain how the game was created, with screenshots and hyperlinks to external sites. It was a triumph for Jake and he revelled in the freedom he had been given, as well as demonstrating his skill, which we all lauded him for.

The sad note of the whole experience happened the following year. Jake moved into Year 5 and was told to design a board game. He and his classmates from my group asked the teacher about creating a computer-based quiz. 'Jake can show us what to do and we can learn to program it. Look at his rainforest one, Miss, it's brilliant!' As you can guess, my colleague had not yet been persuaded by the merits of Unhomework and responded with, 'My plan says you will design a board game, so focus on what you're being asked to do.' But, as the proof of Unhomework's success is how the children carry it out when they're not with you, I was delighted that Jake and the other children I had had in Year 4 completed their board game but also met after school to create a computer game too! When this was shared with my colleague she became a convert to Unhomework, and the next year set 'create a game' as the project, not simply a board game!

Teach others

This was something new I brought to my current school, transferring it from the secondary sector. It worked, as my class always loved seeing how they were compared to secondary school children. One day, in the academic year of 2010, the following exchange happened:

Child 1: So, Mr Creasy, what's the real difference between teaching us and older children?

MC: Well, hmm, actually not much, I suppose.

C 2: You used to tease them too?

MC: Yes, and like you, they gave me a bad back.

C 2: How?

MC: Well, with you it hurts from all the looking down and with them it hurt having to look up as they all towered over me!

C 2: Ha, ha, very funny!

C 1: No, seriously, what's the difference?

MC: (*Realising a glib answer wouldn't cut the mustard*) Probably only three things, I guess.

C 1, 2 and 3: They are?

MC: Okay, well, I can't talk about proper TV programmes with you. We used to have good discussions about sport – especially football. And you don't teach each other or other classes.

C 1: Why can't we?

MC: Why can't you what?

C 1: Teach other classes. I reckon we could.

MC: (*Sensing an opportunity, plus a challenge with other teachers*) What would you teach?

Quick conflab between C 1 and C 2: Anything we want.

C 2: We could see what they need help with and do that.

C 1: Or we could teach each other things we've covered to review our learning and check we know it ourselves.

MC: Okay, but what about the rest of the class?

C 1: They'll love it.

So over break Child 1 and Child 2 had conversations with the other class members and by the time we returned they had a plan formulated. They would all pair up, if they wanted to, and decide what they would deliver and to whom. If it was to another class they would approach the teacher and agree times; if it was to our class they would lead the lesson in its normal slot on the timetable.

Once again my class had managed to surprise me and surpass any expectations I had of them. The teachers were duly approached and the children went to work with Year 2, 3 and our own class, and I had a flurry of emails validating the children's conversations with them. What intrigued me was what the children decided to teach. Two of my quietest girls went to Year 2 and led a PSHE lesson all about bullying and how to treat each other, based on seeing behaviours in the playground. In our own class there were two memorable lessons: John taught multiplication using Roman numerals, to fit in with our Invaders and Settlers topic, and Harry led a lesson in Latin, which he had researched himself.

The two interesting footnotes to this experience were the positive comments from the children – my class and those they taught – and the staff to whom they went. Everyone was amazed at how mature they were and what they managed to deliver. Some even made return visits to the classes and many parents also commented on their efforts and focus to do the best job. To be honest, some of the children were better prepared and resourced than many teachers I have worked with over the years! The second footnote is more personal and goes back to the initial exchange and the breaktime events. As I went to the staffroom the following happened:

Child 3: So what proper TV programmes then?

MC: Pardon?

Child 3: You said you can't chat about proper TV programmes, like what?

MC: Well, *The Apprentice* for a start.

Child 3: I've heard of it, but why's it so good?

MC: Well, firstly you'd see that you lot often behave better than adults. But I think it teaches about getting on, problem solving and everything we use in class.

Child 3: And when's it on?

MC: Wednesday nights, but you'd be in bed.

Child 3: Oh.

The next week, Friday morning:

Child 3: Wasn't *The Apprentice* great, Mr Creasy?

MC: You watched it?

Child 3: I thought you'd appreciate it; I got my Mum to Sky Plus it.

After a conversation about the merits of *The Apprentice*, we struck a deal that I would watch the programme on a Thursday night so we could chat about it on Friday morning in tutor time.

Examples from secondary school children

Revision lessons

In the academic year 2008, I was teaching a GCSE PE class comprising only boys when I was approached by a few of them, asking if they could lead a session in the next theory lesson, as they'd previously found leading a warm-up useful. We discussed what they would like to lead on and they thought that the circulatory system would be best. We agreed that the following week they would prepare a twenty-minute slot, which meant that I would be ready to support them, or intervene if necessary.

When, on the morning of the lesson, the two boys came to me, I'm ashamed to say that I expected the worst of them, especially when they started the conversation with:

Boys: Mr Creasy, we have a problem with our session.

Fortunately, I did not launch into a diatribe about letting me down or anything else I was privately thinking.

MC: What's the problem?

Boys: You see, we did a practice last night with some of the other class and we've planned too much. Can we do the whole lesson?

(*As I recovered myself they continued*): We've planned a starter activity and one of them plenary things. *From their bags they produced a plan and envelopes for the activities, plus a memory stick for the PowerPoint.*

Boys: Is this okay?

MC: Absolutely, but you know the class might not work at the pace you expect so you might not fit it all in.

Boys: No problem, we've worked out what we can cut and even thought of homework.

MC: Really? What?

Boys (*grinning*): Simple. DIY.

MC: DIY?

Boys: Yes, we've led a revision session – now do it yourselves!

The lesson went swimmingly. The boys loved what their peers had done, the best part being that they had thought about how they each learn differently – my references to learning styles and the PLTS had paid off. The homework was then taken up, with each group starting with a quick quiz on prior learning from others, and the activities became more and more detailed to try to 'beat' what others had done.

When we came to reviewing the year, the boys said it was this session that had helped them the most. This was proven by the fact that every single one of them exceeded their target grade and no one achieved less than a grade B – the lowest target had been an E.

Timelines

Having taught English to a variety of abilities over the years, I have found that one element which often eludes them is the context of the text they are studying. This was the case with Steinbeck's *Of Mice and Men* in the academic year 2008. I had to take over a class when a teacher left and I found that this was the text chosen to study – not one of my favourites, but that was beside the point.

Fortunately, I was already taking the majority of the class for maths or PE, so they knew of my Unhomework way of doing things. When we discussed the setting and context of the novel it became clear that they didn't know about the lives George and Lennie would have led. The task was clear: 'Create your own understanding of life at that time.' That was my simple instruction, and we agreed that two weeks would be enough time to complete it (I had thought a week but the class decided on two).

As the first week went past, I heard whispers of some of the tasks they were undertaking, not least from the music department, who asked if I had given permission for four of my class to record a song for English. 'It's about *Of Mice and Men*,' I was told. Of course, I had given no such consent, but told the music teacher otherwise, as tacitly I had agreed that they could do whatever it took to fulfil the task.

On the due date, the class arrived with a variety of pieces as evidence of their understanding:

- A timeline on a roll of wallpaper, painted and decorated with a clear colour code.

- Several PowerPoints, the best being one which hyperlinked with appropriate music from that era which the child had downloaded.

- A card game where the events of the story were represented on each card.

- Two board games where you moved around and answered true or false questions to check your learning about the events.

Then the four children I had heard about stood up and said, 'We haven't got our evidence here, Mr Creasy.' There was clear shock from the class – these children always did what was expected of them, and more. 'Can you all come with us?' When we left the room, they took us (no surprise) to the music practice room; all of their instruments were there and every part of the wall was decorated with images contemporary to the novel. They then proceeded to play their song, which covered the major events at the time, and the lead singer used a laser pointer to highlight the images as she sang about them.

Not only did I love it, so did the class. They got the four children to record it and then they all got copies to listen to, reminding them of the points.

Even better was the open evening a fortnight later – the parents were so impressed with what had been achieved, especially as some of the children were present and could tell them how they did it. They used this inspiration for creating timelines for other texts, but followed the Unhomework ideal of not repeating things they had already done to develop other skills. That led to some other children writing and performing songs based on other Unhomework tasks.

We'll prove you wrong

One of the most heartening examples of Unhomework is the one that occurred during the academic year 2007. It did require more effort from me than usual, but in this case I didn't mind a bit as it was well worth the effort.

I was fortunate enough to be teaching one of those pivotal C/D borderline classes in the maths department. It was filled with children who were very clever but either through laziness, diffidence, attendance or personality clashes with other staff, were not meeting their target grades. If the deterioration from Year 10 continued into Year 11 that would seriously impact on the school's results. However, I was more concerned that a group of children I genuinely liked and who had so much to offer were missing the grade. At the end of the summer term in Year 10, once my Year 11 classes had left, I was given them with the clear remit of 'turning them around'.

As the autumn term commenced, they seriously knuckled down and between them created some amazing examples of Unhomework, including revision notes for each other where they each took responsibility for a topic and provided ideas and prompts for everyone else. I discovered that they had a text/email support chain, where for any given homework they would have four nominated children that the others were able to contact and ask for support when they were stuck. They had instigated two simple rules: a) You can't just tell someone the

answer, and b) You have to ask for specific help, not just say you don't get it. This was in the infancy of implementing Unhomework with this group and, given the composition of the group and the necessity of picking up their grades, homework around exam questions was frequently set. However, by October half-term I stopped doing that as they had set up their own study groups and would meet with questions to set and answer together.

Anyway, the one issue that needed to be addressed was their aggrieved stance at being omitted from taking the statistics paper. It was the most frequent thing that came up during a starter or plenary session when I asked, 'What questions do you have that you can't answer?' It was after almost three weeks of me explaining the department policy, and of them telling me that they were sure I liked to break the rules, that I decided they needed to address the head of department, who reluctantly agreed.

In the next lesson, two children who had been delegated to present their views spoke passionately and with reason for ten minutes about how things were different now; they knew they had not shown their potential previously and this was something they wanted to do. It's fair to say I was bursting with pride at their considered points. If I hadn't already been sold on the idea, I certainly would have been after that. However, I could have thumped the head of department when he simply said, 'Well, you've given it some thought, but the simple fact is you're not in set 1 or 2 and your grades from Year 10 indicate you'll be lucky to pass the maths paper, let alone statistics. The main reason is how will you fit it all in? You've enough to catch up on as it is.'

This led to several children shouting out, claiming he was not listening, and that, essentially, it was his decision to move them all out of sets 1 and 2. During this, one girl just sat with her hand up. As I quelled the storm, I saw she was resolute in having her say. I was glad I asked Jane to speak:

MC: Jane?

Jane: I can see your point. (*Turning to others who protested*) No, I can. We've got ourselves into this mess.

HoD: Thank you for realising that, Jane. I'm glad someone was listening!

Jane: Oh, I was, Sir. You said the main reason was that we couldn't find the time to fit it in, didn't he, Mr Creasy?

MC: Well, yes he did.

HoD: I said other things as well …

Jane: But you did say that, didn't you?

HoD: I did.

Jane: So if we find the time and we prove to you our grades are up to it, you'll let us do it?

HoD: But where will you find the time and how will you prove it?

Jane: Simple, we'll work at lunchtime and all of our mock grades will be at least a C. (*She looked around the class at this point, and spoke with such conviction they all nodded meekly, including my two six-footer rugby boys.*)

HoD: Well, er, I suppose so, but what about the statistics paper?

Jane: We'll agree to sit a mock in February, not the usual December time, which will give us time to learn anything extra we need to, and you'll still have time to enter us because isn't the deadline for entries March, Mr Creasy?

MC: It is.

Jane: Settled then.

HoD: Hmm, but who'll teach you? I won't, if that's what you're thinking!

Jane: It's okay, we'll sort it. And no, Sir, I wasn't thinking you'd teach us.

HoD: Okay.

As the head of department left the room Jane was roundly congratulated, but she just asked if they agreed and were prepared to work. The response wasn't always in the politest language, but it pretty much embodied the sentiment of anything to prove the head of department wrong. 'Mr Creasy ...' said Jane, and I knew what was coming. 'Let's look at a schedule then, shall we?' I replied.

Naturally, they were true to their word, aided by their intrinsic motivation towards proving themselves to the head of department, as well as Jane's useful research revealing that 60% of the statistics paper was already covered in the maths paper and another part could be achieved by the coursework they completed. That left just a little extra to be explained and developed.

Come August 2008, the results day was filled with more anticipation than normal for me. I had every confidence in the children, and despite teaching three other GCSE classes, I was really only focused on the statistics results – and not only because it was the first time I had taught it myself. When I saw the results list, any fears were proved to be unfounded. The children were better than their word: not only had they all passed, but the lowest grade for either the statistics or maths paper was a B, and Jane got an A on both!

I think that all of these examples, from both sectors, show that children can and do take responsibility for themselves. Admittedly, in the last example they needed more input from me than in others, but I think they all demonstrate the necessity and importance of the 5Rs from Chapter 2. Without those and the right climate nothing will flourish, certainly not Unhomework, as the children need to feel the freedom to take it on.

BEYOND UNHOMEWORK

This is designed to provide you with some final points, thoughts and information to support you in developing Unhomework in your own classroom and beyond.

Internet resources

I have found that some of the best Unhomework comes by enticing the children into learning (see Hywel Roberts's excellent *Oops! Helping Children Learn Accidentally* for more on this); 'playing games' is a great way of immersing children in the work so they lose track of time. Most schools will have preferred websites they subscribe to but here are a few you may like. The children will undoubtedly add others to your list.

+ **www.iamlearning.co.uk** – Covers pretty much all subjects with a variety of games, where you can use content already there or set your own – even better if the children do it as well! Set up classes and then watch the competition as they challenge to move up the champions league within a class, school or the entire community.

+ **www.toondoo.com** (registration required) – Does what it says on the tin. Children can create their own online cartoons, which they can then save or print and then share in class to reflect an aspect of learning (it also makes for an effective, yet simple, display!) I have also found it a great tool for supporting planning for story writing in English, especially for those who may claim they can't draw!

+ **www.bbc.co.uk** – This is a huge site, and there is much to be said for a serendipitous trawl through it. However, the subject-specific areas of the site are great for stimulating the children's interests or developing knowledge based on what you've covered in class. I have always taught children the need to be specific in terms of what they are searching for, whilst not being too prescriptive with the words they use in any search to ensure the widest possible options.

Some specific areas I use:

http://www.bbc.co.uk/learningzone/clips

http://www.bbc.co.uk/programmes/b037mkj3/features/how-to-guides http://www.bbc.co.uk/learning/schoolradio (for free podcasts) http://www.bbc.co.uk/bitesize – this one is applicable across the age ranges and not just in the summer term when exams loom. I have also found this is a great resource for some reluctant readers (especially boys), who will spend hours poring over the football news and statistics, then share this in class!

+ **www.triptico.co.uk** – A great teaching resource for staff. Certain applications are ideal for Unhomework, especially 'What's in the box?' Also, children can create their own 'Match it' cards (I have had the problem of having too many sets as they all enjoy creating them, so be warned!)

+ **www.edmodo.com** (registration required) – This is a simple site that allows for easy communication between staff and classes, where they can not only post work but pose questions and collaborate interactively. In fact, last year's Invaders and Settlers project was conducted almost entirely through this site so the children could discuss the work outside of class; they could upload their work for their group to comment on, or just share ideas with other groups.

Books to support Unhomework

I love gaining inspiration from others, so much of which has supported and developed Unhomework since I started it in my classes. The 5Rs and the aspirations I have set out in the previous chapters have all been supported and encouraged by the writings that I have listed below, as well as those in my bibliography. This is especially true as I have been fortunate enough to see some of these writers in person and communicate with them over time. I highly recommend their works to develop anyone's classroom practice.

This is obviously not an exhaustive list, however, I have tried to share with you those whose writings have affected my personal classroom practice and allowed me to arrive at my own book.

Dewey, John (2012 – reprint of 1910 edition) *How We Think*. Martino Publishing.

Dweck, Carol (2006) *Mindset: The New Psychology of Success*. Ballantine Books.

Gladwell, Malcolm (2002) *The Tipping Point: How Little Things Can Make a Big Difference*. Abacus Books.

Gladwell, Malcolm (2006) *Blink: The Power of Thinking Without Thinking*. Penguin Books.

Gladwell, Malcolm (2009) *Outliers: The Story of Success*. Penguin Books.

Kahneman, Daniel (2012) *Thinking, Fast and Slow*. Penguin Books.

Kelley, Paul (2007) *Making Minds: What's Wrong With Education and What Should We Do About It?* Routledge Books.

Personal, Learning and Thinking Skills

Independent enquirers	Reflective learners
I can:	I can:
+ process information	+ see my strengths
+ plan how to use information	+ set myself goals to improve
+ make informed decisions	+ check my own progress
+ see other people have different beliefs to me	+ use feedback to make changes
I will:	I will:
+ think of problems to tackle	+ see opportunities for myself
+ think ahead about how my plans might work out	+ set my own success criteria
+ plan my own research	+ ask for feedback
+ explore problems from more than one viewpoint	+ accept praise and criticism
+ analyse information	+ assess myself
+ judge the value of all information	+ use experiences to improve future progress
+ think how feelings and beliefs influence events	+ communicate in different ways
+ use arguments and evidence for my views	

Self-managers

I can:
+ organise and be responsible for myself
+ show initiative and be creative
+ be committed to self-improvement
+ cope with challenges

I will:
+ seek out new challenges and responsibilities
+ be flexible if things change
+ show perseverance
+ organise my time and resources
+ take risks
+ manage different pressures
+ be positive about changes
+ ask for advice and support when I need it
+ build and maintain relationships

Team workers

I can:
+ work confidently with others
+ take on different roles in groups
+ listen to others
+ compromise my views with others

I will:
+ work with others towards a set goal
+ change my behaviour based on my role
+ take on leadership roles
+ be confident in myself and my value to the group
+ be fair and considerate to others
+ be responsible for myself
+ give support and feedback to others

Creative thinkers	Effective participators
I can:	I can:
• explore ideas	• play a full part in school life
• make connections between ideas	• engage with issues affecting me and others
• tackle problems in different ways	• take responsible actions
• work with others to find solutions	• bring improvements for others
I will:	I will:
• ask questions to explore ideas	• discuss my concerns
• explore different outcomes	• work with others to find solutions
• connect my ideas to the ideas of others	• suggest ways to solve problems
• ask questions of my own ideas	• identify improvements for others
• challenge the thinking of other people	• negotiate with others
• adapt my ideas as things change	• listen to a range of views
	• balance my views with those of others
	• stand up for views different to my own

MISSION: HOMEWORK

Your target up to half-term is to earn a *minimum* of 100 points. You will achieve this by selecting homework tasks from those below. You can choose to do **any** of these tasks, to meet or exceed the total points.

The focus is *quality work*, not just completing tasks quickly (you have three weeks!) Think carefully about the presentation and content of your work to make sure you give your best to produce work you can be proud of.

You are a Roman soldier; write a letter home telling your family how great or awful Britain is. **30 points**	Design a fierce Viking ship prow figurehead. **10 points** Add an explanation of your picture to gain another: **10 points**	Plan a Roman themed party for your class. Include games, food and decorations. **60 points**
Research and present a fact file about a Roman emperor of your choice. **20 points**	Design a t-shirt and cuddly toy to be sold in a museum for an invader/ settler of your choice. **30 points**	Write an acrostic poem for: invader, settler, electricity or skeleton – ensure it relates to the word you have used. **20 points**

Write a war song for your chosen set of invaders. **20 points** Compose the music for another: **20 points**	Design a Science poster titled 'Electrical Safety' or 'How the Body Works'. Include text and diagrams. **10 points**	Design a website homepage for any topic you have studied this term. Include the links you would have. **30 points**
Make a Roman mosaic. **20 points** Make the mosaic link to another subject for a bonus: **20 points**	Design a word search for any subject. **10 points** Write questions so people find the answers for a bonus: **20 points**	Write a newspaper front page about the Viking/Roman invasion, Moses freeing the Israelites or Noah's Ark. **30 points** *continued …*
Design a stained glass window for any of the Bible stories you have looked at in RE. **20 points**	Design a range of Lego figures for one of the invader/settler civilisations you have looked at. **20 points**	Make and label a model to demonstrate your learning in any subject from this term. **30 points**
Bonus points Create any other work to earn a minimum of **20 points** per piece of work.		

BIBLIOGRAPHY

Beadle, P. (2008) *Could Do Better: Help Your Kid Shine At School.* London, Corgi Books.

Beadle, P. (2010) *How to Teach.* Carmarthen, Crown House Publishing.

Beadle, P. (2011) *Dancing About Architecture: A Little Book of Creativity.* Carmarthen, Crown House Publishing.

Curran, A. (2008) *The Little Book of Big Stuff About the Brain.* Carmarthen, Crown House Publishing.

Dewey, J. (2012 edn) *How We Think.* Eastford, CT, Martino Publishing.

Dweck, C. (2006) *Mindset: The New Psychology of Success.* New York, Ballantine Books.

Elder, Z. (2013) *Full on Learning: Involve Me and I'll Understand.* Carmarthen, Crown House Publishing.

Friedman, T. L. (2007) *The World is Flat.* London. Penguin Books.

Gilbert, I. (2002) *Essential Motivation in the Classroom.* Abingdon, Routledge.

Gilbert, I. (2010) *Why Do I Need a Teacher When I've Got Google?* Abingdon, Routledge.

Gladwell, M. (2002) *The Tipping Point: How Little Things Can Make a Big Difference.* London, Abacus Books.

Gladwell, M. (2006) *Blink: The Power of Thinking Without Thinking.* London, Penguin Books.

Gladwell, M. (2009) *Outliers: The Story of Success.* London, Penguin Books.

Griffith, A. and Burns, M. (2012) *Engaging Learners.* Carmarthen, Crown House Publishing.

Heathcote, D. and Bolton, G. (1996) *Drama for Learning: Dorothy Heathcote's Mantle of the Expert Approach to Education.* London, Heinemann.

Jackson, N. (2009) *The Little Book of Music for the Classroom*. Carmarthen, Crown House Publishing.

Jensen, E. (2008) *Super Teaching: Over 1000 Practical Strategies*. Newbury Park, CA, Corwin Press.

Kahneman, D. (2012) *Thinking, Fast and Slow*. London, Penguin Books.

Keeling, D. and Hodgson, D. (2011) *Invisible Teaching: 101 Ways to Create Energy, Openness and Focus in the Classroom*. Carmarthen, Crown House Publishing.

Kelley, P. (2008) *Making Minds: What's Wrong With Education – and What Should We Do About It?* Abingdon, Routledge.

Mandela, N. (1994) *Long Walk to Freedom*. London, Abacus Books.

Masten, A. S. (2009) Ordinary magic: lessons from research on resilience in human development. *Education Canada* 49 (3): 28–32.

Masten, A. S. and Wright, M. O'D. (2009) 'Resilience over the lifespan: developmental perspectives on resistance, recovery, and transformation'. In J. W. Reich,

A. J. Zautra and J. S. Hall (eds.), *Handbook of Adult Resilience*. New York, Guilford Press.

Powell, R. (1997) *Active Whole-Class Teaching*. Rochester, Robert Powell Publications

Roberts, H. (2012) *Oops! Helping Children Learn Accidentally*. Carmarthen, Independent Thinking Press.

Ryan, W. (2011) *Inspirational Teachers, Inspirational Learners: A Book of Hope for Creativity and the Curriculum in the Twenty-First Century*. Carmarthen, Crown House Publishing.

Smith, J. (2010) *The Lazy Teacher's Handbook: How Your Students Learn More When You Teach Less*. Carmarthen. Crown House Publishing.

WEBOGRAPHY

Abbott, J. (2010) The making of teachers, *The 21st Century Learning Initiative*. http://www.21learn.org/uncategorized/the-making-of-teachers/

BBC Newsround (2012) Government scraps homework rules for English schools (5 March). http://www.bbc.co.uk/newsround/17255075

Corbett, S. (2012) Walter Dean Myers named national Ambassador for Young People's Literature (3 January). http://www.publishersweekly.com/pw/by-topic/childrens/childrens-industry-news/article/50033-walter-dean-myers-named-nationalambassador-for-young-people-s-literature.html

Dumb Ways to Die (2012) http://www.youtube.com/watch?v=IJNR2EpS0jw

Henry, J. (2012) Michael Gove scraps homework rules, *The Telegraph* (3 March). http://www.telegraph.co.uk/education/9121048/Michael-Gove-scraps-homework-rules.html

Heathcote, D. (n.d.) *Mantle of the Expert*. http://www.mantleoftheexpert.com

Cupaiuolo, C. (n.d.) Playback: making media, engaging in democracy, and working toward the future. http://spotlight.macfound.org/blog/entry/playback-making-media-engaging-in-democracyworking-toward-the-future/

Independent Thinking (n.d.) 8Way Thinking. http://www.independentthinking.co.uk/Cool+Stuff/8Way+Thinking/default.aspx

Qualifications and Curriculum Authority (2008)
A big picture of the curriculum. http://webarchive.
nationalarchives.gov.uk/20080806121643/http://qca.
org.uk/libraryAssets/media/Big_Picture_2008.pdf

Shift Happens (2008) http://www.youtube.com/
watch?v=FdTOFkhaplo

Sundem, G. (2012) Homework in the home,
Psychology Today (28 February). http://www.
psychologytoday.com/blog/brain-trust/201202/
homework-help-hurts-learning

Walker, J. M. T, Hoover-Dempsey, K. V., Whetsel,
D. R. and Green, C. L. (2004) Parental involvement
in homework: a review of current research and its
implications for teachers, after school program staff, and
parent leaders, *Harvard Family Research Project*. http://
www.gse.harvard.edu/hfrp/projects/fine/resources/
research/homework.html

CONTACT ME

Increasingly, in recent years, I have found that through electronic communications I have been able to share and discuss a great deal with colleagues, picking up true nuggets of excellence to use, as well as some plain nuggets! If you'd like to contact me to discuss things further, you can find me on Twitter at:

www.twitter.com/EP3577

(To put you out of your misery with decoding my address: I'm a huge Elvis fan – Elvis Presley, 1935–1977.)

Good luck and happy Unhomeworking! Remember the wise words of Abraham Lincoln,

'When I do good, I feel good. When I do bad, I feel bad!'

This sounds like the perfect mission statement for Unhomework to me!

Homework, homework, homework. As a teacher it can sometimes feel that you're damned if you do, or damned if you don't, set enough. Some parents complain that you are setting far too much – others complain that their child needs more! Setting a 'creative' project for homework will get many parents scrambling for cereal boxes as they make a model in the same vein as *Blue Peter*'s Tracy Island model back in the 1990s – usually the night before the project is due; whereas other parents leave their children to it – you can generally tell the disparity.

We have discussed the purpose of homework previously on UKEdChat when we explored the question, 'Is homework a vital learning tool or an outdated educational throwback?' concluding that if children are asked to work at home, the activity should be useful and relevant to their school work, allowing pupils to follow their interests and passions to instil a love of learning and it should indulge their curiosity using their creativity to push their learning forward. Fire up your class with stimulating collaborative projects which will be enjoyed by both child and parent. Let 'will this light them up?' be our mantra.

There usually are two schools of thought regarding homework: on the one hand, let children be children. They spend enough hours sat down motionless in school. Let them play and explore the world: on the other hand, homework should extend the learning children do at school, reinforcing concepts explored. Schools will have homework policies, which vary wildly in the amount of homework teachers are expected to assign, however there will be very few schools that have an 'Unhomework' policy – the philosophy advocated by teacher Mark Creasy, which ensures that the work students complete outside the classroom is relevant, purposeful and engaging for them, no matter the age of the pupils. The main assumption with the Unhomework philosophy is that children are inspired to complete it without being told to do so. It is always pleasurable when pupils come into school sharing a project that they have done, as they are inspired by their learning or topic – with no homework task set.

The philosophy works at all stages of school education, with Creasy stating that he has taught children aged 8–18 with his approach being no different, although he does concede that secondary pupils need more support and encouragement as it is a different approach to what they are used to.

The book supports teachers in developing this philosophy – which many primary colleagues already pursue – introducing the DAD Model, which is essentially a more discussion or collaborative-based formula for home tasks, including: tips on getting parents on-board with the philosophy; convincing colleagues; developing the concept as a whole-school project plus a collection of ideas and tips to create ideas and put them into action.

This book is a great supporter for how homework should be – a pleasurable experience for pupils, parents and teachers. It should not be a chore, but an activity that consolidates, extends or enthuses pupils further in the learning experience.

Book reviewer, UKEDChat e-zine

The contents of this book are dear to my heart and remind me of similar initiatives I promoted as a primary school teacher and head over the past 30 years.

I applaud the author for a really practice-based account of introducing a new philosophy of home-based learning. Not only has his approach raised standards of attainment and self-esteem in his pupils but also introduced a family learning basis for homework.

Being inspired by others is one of the most impressive effects of this work and I can recommend it as a primer for teachers wishing to promote independent learning, resilience and family involvement in their classrooms.

Susan Drecksler M.Ed CPCC

Mark Creasy is absolutely correct in his assessment of homework; it must have value, purpose and authenticity to students. The students should take the content in the direction that interests and gives power to them so they become invested in the learning process. Once this investing occurs the learning becomes authentic. The teacher's role is to provide support, feedback, structure and expansion of the student-directed learning – this is the main premise of Unhomework.

The struggles with parents that Creasy describes are all too common. Parents and other adults believe that because they went to school – the accidental apprenticeship of teaching – they understand education today. These stakeholders want their children to have similar educational experiences – homework, traditional homework (e.g. 'Complete math problems 1–48 on page 124'; 'Write your vocabulary words 10 times and place in a complete sentence', etc.). Parents fail to understand that things have changed when it comes to learning – the process, the tolls, the instructional methods and the resources – we as educators need to adapt to the change and continue to 'push the envelope' as we educate our children. Mark Creasy is spot on in his process and the concept of 'supported failure'; this makes mistakes and errors OK, as they are used as a new starting point – not a road block to success. True educators support students through failures and demonstrate tenacity to their students.

Dr Shawn DiNarda Watters, Assistant Professor and Paraprofessional Program Coordinator, Wayne College, University of Akron

---

This is a book which should be read by anybody involved in education, from parents who wish to know how to support their children's learning, to government ministers who desire to solve the country's apparent falling behind in academic league tables in recent years.

I've taught in a number of schools, both state and independent, in this country and overseas, and homework has always been an issue which causes controversy. In many cases, it's a necessary evil for teachers, a source of misery for children and exasperation for parents. But this is not how homework, and indeed learning, should be. Mark's philosophy for the way children learn makes total common sense.

The book clearly sets out the reasoning behind Unhomework, as well as the methods by which it can be applied in both the primary and secondary sector. Success stories of how it has been used are an inspiration and I was eager to start using some of Mark's ideas with my class before I'd even finished the book. As a parent, I also found the section on how parents can get involved very interesting. My daughter is just a toddler, but I'm sure Mark (and many parents and educators for that matter) would agree with me in the belief that it's never too early to encourage creativity and develop learning skills.

The chapter on how to convince colleagues is an interesting one based on Mark's experience. We teachers work very long hours and often feel like we're struggling to just keep afloat. I know we can torture ourselves by thinking we've still not done enough and if only we had a few more hours in the day ... In adopting Unhomework, once you've taken the time to really get the hang of it and ensure your pupils do too, I can see this burden would be somewhat lifted. And of course the results are children who want to learn, who want to do their best, who want to achieve their goals and who ultimately get better results.

I could see Unhomework working in any of the schools I've taught in. I'm currently both a class and MFL teacher and after reading this, wished I was responsible for 'setting' more homework than I currently do! However, it's not just about homework; it's about a learning philosophy that can be applied in our teaching really quite simply and without a great deal of onerous work, as can often be the case.

Zoe Atkins, MFL Teacher

978-1-78135-009-6

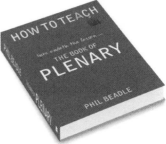

978-1-78135-053-9

www.independentthinkingpress.com